Barry Manilow is a superstar! His rise from commercial jingles to platinum records is phenomenal.

Read all about his dazzling career; his days with Bette Midler; his back-up group, Lady Flash; his beagle, Bagel!

Complete discography and astrological chart included!

BARRY MANILOW

An Unauthorized Biography
by Mark Bego

tempo
books

GROSSET & DUNLAP
A FILMWAYS COMPANY
Publishers • New York

To Bob & Mary:
Who thought that all I could write
was home . . . for money!

BARRY MANILOW
Copyright © 1977 by Mark Bego
All rights reserved
Published simultaneously in Canada

ISBN: 0-448-14550-2
A Tempo Books Original
Tempo Books is registered in the U.S. Patent Office

Printed in the United States of America

ACKNOWLEDGMENTS

Extra special thanks to these special people:

IRV BEIGEL • MONICA BURRUSS • DEBRA BYRD • DON ELAM • LEE GURST • DON KIRSHNER • BARRY MANILOW • MARTHA REEVES • REPARATA

Special appreciation and thanks to:

AL ALTMAN • BOBBY BANK • CATHERINE BEGO • NANCY BEGO • HOWARD BLOOM • MIKE CAPLAN • JACK CUNNINGHAM • LARA DONIN • ALYSS DO-RESE • EILEEN FULTON • DON GILLESPIE • PETER GLANKOFF • REN GREVATT • JO HAYDEN • LENORE HERSON • MARY HILTON • WALTER KOLES • IDA LANGSAM • ROBIN LONDON • SUE McDONALD • C.C.H. POUNDER • PAT RIVALGI • RICHIE ROTHEN-STEIN • RITA SALK • CHERYL SCHWARTZ • MARK STERN • TODD WEINSTEIN • SHARON WEISZ

Love to MY amazing back-up ladies:

BARBRA NAGEL • BARBARA SHELLEY • MARSHA STERN • BETH WERNICK

. . . and thanks to Yings Chinese . . . for delivering!

CONTENTS

Prologue

While piecing together "the Barry Manilow story" contained in these pages, I was not only concerned with the task of presenting the contributing facts, dates, and occurrences that led up to his tremendous success; but I was also fascinated by the many diverse dimensions that his career has already encompassed. In addition to having interviewed Barry himself, I turned to some of the key personalities in Manilow's life for insight and directional assistance.

I talked to his back-up group, Lady Flash, about touring and recording with Barry; I discussed his commercial career with his drummer and long-time friend Lee Gurst; I delved into his development years with Irv Biegel who is responsible for Manilow's first recording contract; and I even consulted with astrologer Don Elam to see what looms in the artist's future! When I had assembled all of my data, I felt that I wanted to take my observations one step further to obtain a more complete biographical composite, so I sought the sound advice of the music industry's Number One audio apostle and pop prophet . . . Don Kirshner.

"I loved him because he had a scope and a depth to him," remembers Don of the first time that he heard Barry sing and play the piano. The interview had been in Kirshner's New York office, and at the time Manilow was auditioning as a writer for Don's creative pool which had already yielded over the years such artists as Neil Sedaka, Carole King, and Neil Diamond among others.

"The songs he played me were not 'I Write The Songs' or 'Mandy' or anything like that . . . which were fine. I thought he needed work, I thought he needed experience and development, and I liked him a lot."

In the same office, some twenty-eight floors above the roar of the city, I sat in a soft armchair in front of Don's desk and surveyed the surrounding walls covered with "Gold" Records and glass-framed rock memorabilia. Although many people recognize Don as the host/producer of television's popular weekly "Don Kirshner's Rock Concert" and annual "Rock Awards," many still fail to realize that he began in the late fifties as a song-writer with partner Bobby Darin. In the sixties, Donnie, as his friends call him, conceived of, cast, and produced The Monkees through a television show, three "Number One" singles, and millions of albums. With his accumulated publishing rights, he has been directly responsible for the sales of over 200 million records either as publisher or record company head.

Kirshner pointed out that he had first encountered the decade's star pianist through one of his company's staff producers, Ron Dante.

"Ron of course did 'Sugar, Sugar' for me, and he now produces Manilow.

"Ron always used to talk about Barry Manilow," Don recalls. "And, when Bette Midler opened, I went with Ronny and his wife to see her, and Barry was conducting in the background. He brought Barry in one day, and Barry proceeded to play me two or three songs ... which I thought were 'O.K.' I was about to sign Barry as a writer, and his deal was too tough, he wanted half of the publishing rights. This was at the period he was doing commercials, and I knew him from the streets with all of the other kids.

"I said, 'We can't make a deal,' and eventually he signed with Clive Davis and Artista Records. But, what was interesting, inside of that ... we stayed friendly."

Glancing to one of the "Gold" recordings on the wall, Kirshner reflects, "Barry came in and I played him what I thought would be the next 'Number One' record in the country. He came in with Ronny; and the record was 'Love Will Keep Us Together' (published by 'Don Kirshner Entertainment'). He was sitting right here," he said pointing to the plush chair next to mine before his desk, "and he said, 'I like it ... good hook; great changes on that.' I said 'Yeah, I think it's going to be one of the biggest records in the country!' "

Projecting into Barry's future in recordings, television, and even movies, Kirshner comments on Manilow: "Conquering TV, conquering music, I think Barry, because of the way he looks, and his sensitivity ... that puts him in a different class again! He could play a psychopathic killer, and it would be great; or he could play a gentleman, and it would be great; he could play the kid who is a rebel like in 'Easy Rider.' It has to be the part, but anyone can happen with the right vehicle. He obviously is bright, he's got a lot of stage presence, he knows how to handle people, he's paid his dues; so I think he can make it."

Don Kirshner continues, "Certainly if you put him on Broadway tomorrow, he would probably be giant in the right script, or the right part! That's really the excitement of this business, to sit and see a kid come in and play the piano . . . and the next time you see him, he's the biggest star in the country! So it is very, very exciting!"

On that note: "Ladies and gentlemen, presenting Mr. Barry Manilow . . . "

—Mark Bego
October 1977

I
THE EARLY YEARS
Up from the Jingles ... on to the Singles!

In the short span of four years, Barry Manilow has successfully made the transition from total obscurity and hamburger jingles to Broadway shows and "Gold" singles! At the age of thirty-one, the six-foot-tall music buff from Brooklyn is the most popular singer, composer, pianist to emerge in decades. His recordings have kept his name on the national music charts for three years *solid,* as Barry constantly eclipses himself.

With one "Gold" and four "Platinum" albums to his credit, Barry is presently riding high on an unbeatable winning streak. For eight weeks in the spring and summer of 1977, Barry had the rare distinction as a soloist of having five albums appearing on the Billboard Magazine charts simultaneously. This unique task is a feat only previously accomplished by Frank Sinatra and Johnny Mathis.

Beginning with the release of the song "Mandy" in the fall of 1974, each of his singles have become sure-fire chart toppers. After "Mandy" hit "Number One," subsequent songs such as, "It's a Miracle," "Could It Be Magic?," "I Write The Songs," "Tryin' To Get The Feeling Again," "This One's For You," "Weekend In New England," and "I Think We Made It," have helped make

5

Manilow one of the top drawing box office performers around.

In April, 1977, Barry completed a much publicized "98 city" national tour, which ended in Barry's debut headlining engagement in Las Vegas, at The M.G.M. Grand Hotel. His itinerary included a two-week S.R.O. (standing-room-only) sold-out booking on Broadway, at New York's Uris Theater. Barry's fifth album, released during May, 1977 is a collection of "Barry Manilow Live" tapes compiled from his Christmas, 1976 Broadway stage presentation. Certified "Platinum" by the Record Industry Association of America (R.I.A.A.) for sales of 1,000,000 units, the album was at one point, that summer, the "Number One" album in the country.

On March 2, 1977, ABC-TV broadcast the first "Barry Manilow" television special to the American viewing public. The show was seen by over 35 million people, topping all network competition for that time slot.* A spring 1978 special is due to break further video records.

In the early seventies Barry began his professional singing and writing career on television commercials for various products including Kentucky Fried Chicken, Band-Aids, and State Farm Insurance. A medley of his best-known jingles still draws a fantastic response in his live performances, and is showcased as Barry's "V.S.M." or "Very Strange Medley."

In the spring of 1972, after doing musical arrangements for countless aspiring vocalists, Barry took a job as a piano player in New York's

*This program was the recipient of the 1977 Emmy for Best Musical Variety Show.

Continental Baths. Two weeks later, in walked Bette Midler, ready to be discovered by Barry and the world. In no time Barry had become Bette's pianist, arranger and producer, and she soon afterward landed a recording contract and a national tour. Barry co-produced her first album "The Divine Miss M," and toured with her through the first part of 1973. When they returned to Manhattan, Barry was soon working on a recording contract of his own!

By the fall of 1973, Bette had become the fastest rising star of the seventies, and Barry, who had just released his own debut album, was right there with her! All of the way across the country they toured again, but this time Barry was opening the second act of the show. For the first time he was on the stage alone . . . and much to his surprise, the crowd loved him! The tour ended with three sold-out weeks at New York's Palace Theater, and Bette, together with Barry, had their first dose of Broadway encores and cheering ovations.

As 1974 began, Barry and Bette parted professionally, each to pursue their own career projects. By that fall and the release of the single, "Mandy," from Barry's second album, "Barry Manilow II," the country was suddenly interested in rediscovering that striking piano player they had heard on Bette's first two albums and had seen lurking behind the keyboard in her shows.

Barry's personality is sincere, warm and good-natured, and his main professional intention has always been to lead the listening masses back to what he calls "intelligent music." Today he is an acknowledged media "star" of popular recording and performing. Twice the "Record of the Year" nominee for Grammy Awards, on June 5, 1977

Barry was honored with a "special" Tony Award for his Broadway headlining, and three months later, on September 11, his televised hour was in line to net an Emmy statuette from the TV industry. With the fantastic "cross-over" success of both his first headlining Broadway show and television special in addition to his phenomenal record sales, Manilow has yet to fully realize his career's entire scope!

As with Barry, individuals who are born between May 21 and June 20 are governed by the third sign of Zodiacal influence and are signified by the constellation known as "Gemini, the Twins." Unpredictability is one of the key characteristics of the Gemini personality and individuals born under this sign can change their mind, clothes, occupation, residence or personal life without a moment's notice.

Much to the frustration of those around them, friends of a Gemini will attest to the fact that they know no fewer than two completely different people housed in one Gemini body. A Gemini, however, will always know what it is that he wants . . . at least for the time being. Tomorrow it could be something totally different, but their determination of attainment will be equally as strong.

Gemini is known as a "Mutable/Air" sign. The characteristic denoted by "Mutable" is an alternating changeability between fast-acting and spontaneous, and deliberate and difficult to move. The element of "Air" makes Gemini seek change and communication.

A Gemini should never be backed into a corner topically, as they'll talk a blue streak around any of your arguments. Their verbal acrobatics can leave you convinced that the sun rises in the west if that is their intention. A Gemini is never wrong . . . just ask one.

They are impatient and have the capacity to tackle twelve different projects at once. They are intent upon being the first to be informed; a Gemini can rarely finish half a book before reading the last page of it.

As deemed by the planet Mercury, a Gemini's mentality is always active, versatile, inventive, logical, inquisitive, studious, dispassionate, and categorical. Their method of expression is witty, voluble, humorous, and rational. Their adaptability is instinctive and continuous; their perceptions, rapid and easily-stimulated.

At the same time, the planet Mars adds influence to make the Gemini's desires spontaneous; their energy, nervous; attitude, restless; and method, in inspirational flashes. In love, the Gemini is analytical and careful. From the planet Saturn comes the "motivating fear" of those born under the Twins: being tied down to anything.

As would a bird, these flighty creatures will fly into a room and perch themselves in a seat of optimum visual vantage. Analytically they will peck at only the most important seeds of conversation and have again taken to the air before anyone in the room notices that they've moved a feather.

A Gemini has a way with words. They are a natural in the business world as writers, promoters, and salesmen. Quoth Gemini-born writer Walt Whitman argumentatively, "Do I contradict myself? Very well then I contradict myself!"

On June 17, 1946, one such Gemini was born in Brooklyn, New York. With a quicksilver mind and

Mercury-traced energies Barry Manilow was on a path that would lead him to convince the entire country of his musical merit.

An only child, Barry lived with his family in a not-too-attractive section of Brooklyn. His father deserted the family when Barry was two, but he has only fond memories.

"I come from Division Avenue in Williamsburg—oh, it's so painful! Roots are really the strangest thing to talk about, I'm a definite slum kid; but though I got beaten up a lot by the kids on the block, I lived in a very nice house, and I was treated terrifically by my parents and grandparents, and I never knew I was a slum kid.

"I was into music when I was a kid," Barry remembers. In Times Square in 1948 Barry and his Grandpa, Joe Manilow, went into one of those old coin-operated "Make-A-Record" machines that frequent amusement arcades. On the scratchy waxing Grandpa Joe prods microphone-shy Barry, "Sing it . . . sing 'Happy Birthday . . . Don't you want to make a record? . . ." Barry has obviously shed his fear of recording. That same record from Times Square, on which Barry utters only a handful of syllables, opens Side One of the album "Barry Manilow I."

Barry's introduction to music came at an early age.

"It was the Andrews Sisters when I was three years old, with my mother bopping around the house." Later on, "We kids," Manilow recalls of the old neighborhood gang, "listened to rock and roll on the candy store juke box and harmonized on street corners."

His first instrumental experimentation was at the

age of seven. It was at that time that he began taking accordion lessons.

That first concert at Town Hall left the most lasting impression on him. "When I was thirteen years old my stepfather introduced me to 'intelligent' music by taking me to a Gerry Mulligan-Art Farmer concert. I still remember the concert as if it were yesterday." His first favorite pianists were drawn from the jazz world as well.

"I was raised to get a job and collect that pay check every week, but even if I couldn't be doing what I'm doing now, I'd still be in music somehow even if I had to sweep floors in a recording studio," Barry recalls of his upbringing being on the practical side. "When it came time to decide what I was going to do with my life, I knew music was going to be a part, but I didn't want to take the gamble of actually deciding to make music my living. I could not believe, first of all, that it could be done. Secondly, that I could do it. I thought I would starve in a matter of months. So, I decided to go to a city college for advertising and still play music on weekends. I got so bored learning about marketing, merchandising, and textiles that I finally told myself, 'Aw, come on an' give music a try.'

He attended the New York College of Music and then transferred to Juilliard where he spent two semesters.

After his jazz-influenced stage, Barry's tastes, too, shifted. "Then rock and roll began to creep in. But for a while I never paid much attention to it. I really did not like 'Rock Around The Clock.'" Into the sixties things began to develop along the right lines. "I think the Beatles finally convinced me there was something going on in rock. I said, 'Hold

it, would you run that by me again?' After that rock
got better—better than the same old four chords,
which never really turned me on. And Laura Nyro's
'Eli' album—that was a great influence on my
songwriting."

While he completed his studies, a job working in
the CBS mailroom helped to pay the rent. During
his days at CBS he made a couple of his most
significant acquaintances. The first one was Linda
Allen who is now his general manager and constant
companion. Linda was working in the program-
ming department and gave him the opportunity to
arrange some new music for the theme of the local
station's "Late Show," replacing the outdated
standard, Leroy Anderson's "Syncopated Clock."
The second person that Barry met with a job opportunity was a director who asked eighteen-year-
old Manilow to do some arrangements for a
production of his. This led to working on a musical
version of the stage play "The Drunkard." Barry
did arranging on some public domain songs for it,
and by the time the task was over, he had written a
score and inserted additional original material. The
play ran for six years Off-Off Broadway and for
two years Off Broadway.

During this expanse of time came a typical dis-
play of Gemini changeability with Barry running
through the quicksilver romance of a marriage and
almost as abrupt a divorce.

"I tried it, and I didn't like it," says Barry on the
subject of matrimony. "I didn't have a good time. I
had to come home to the same person all the time
and I didn't want to, even though I might have
loved her. I don't see any reason to get married." He
returns to the present and adds, "My mother and

stepfather got divorced and then started to live really happily. They actually date, and they live together when they feel like it. That seems to me the way to do it."

While he was at CBS, working in the mailroom and going to school at night, Barry suddenly took off for six months to pursue a show business career. He ended up back at CBS one more time before devoting all of his time to music. He became musical director of a weekly series that showcased young talent, "Callback." It was on the air for two seasons and won an Emmy citation.

"Then I got a call from the Ed Sullivan people, asking me to be music director for a series of new pilots they were doing after the Sullivan show went off the air. That was my big network conducting debut."

Manilow's own playing and arranging career was simultaneously sprouting. As he tells it, "I had become pretty good. I really worked at arranging and playing for singers, and I was able to get a lot of work. I was making a decent living and I loved it. I was accompanying just about every singer in town, in clubs and for auditions, for fifteen bucks an hour."

Today Barry is on both sides of the fence, trading hats between the positions of 'singer' and 'arranger.' As he explains, "It's a definite advantage, but not an absolute necessity. For a singer, it's not difficult to learn a new arrangement just from hearing it a couple of times, memorizing it; he or she wouldn't have to know how to read music. For an arranger, though, it's important to understand all the possibilities of every instrument you're dealing with and know how to write music too. It would be hard to arrange without knowing how to write and read music, but I suppose it could be done."

While simultaneously coaching and arranging for singers, Barry wrote a song that one of the vocalists put on a demonstration tape that he took around to different commercial agencies in hopes of landing singing work on an ad. Not only did they like the singer, but they also asked where the song came from, and were given Barry's phone number. He began writing them and eventually found his way into the vocalizing as well.

"It was better than playing in bars," Barry remembers of his transition to recording, "and gave me the opportunity to get into studio work. Even then, I realized that I began to make even more money singing in commercials than I did for writing them!"

Since becoming a popular figure in modern music, there has been much confusion as to which commercials have and have not been written and/or sung by him. Here is a breakdown:

Kentucky Fried Chicken—Sang (original)
Bowlene Toilet Cleaner—Wrote, arranged
State Farm Insurance—Wrote
Stridex—Wrote, sang
Chevrolet—Wrote, sang, arranged
Dr. Pepper—Sang
Pepsi—Sang
Jack-InThe-Box—Sang (original)
MacDonald's—Sang (original)
Band-Aids—Wrote, arranged

It was around this same period that Barry was

hit by a veritable harmonizing hurricane of energy known as Bette Midler.

"It was hate at first sight . . . but we rehearsed anyway, and Saturday night came, and there I was at the Continental Baths in a roomful of naked men and towels, and Bette came on stage looking like my mother with a fox around her neck and a turban on her head. I was rolling under the piano.

When Barry first checked into the job at the Continental Baths in the spring of 1972, he figured that he was simply going to end up as a sub at the tubs. It wasn't long, however, before the transition was made from bath-house tiles to concert-hall aisles. Bette and her newly formed act found itself in immediate demand, first for an engagement at the Upstairs At The Downstairs—and then on to a recording contract for Bette, and more studio experience for Barry.

What came out of the Atlantic Recording Studios at the end of December, 1972, was a classic album for Bette entitled, "The Divine Miss M." Certified "Gold" and later nominated for an "Album of The Year" Grammy Award, it established her as an overnight sensation and was a fabulous credit for Barry and the other talented performers who make contributions to this divine disc.

On "Do You Want To Dance?" Barry is featured on the piano, Ralph MacDonald does percussion work and a string and horn section, and Cissy Houston is among the back-up vocalists. Ralph MacDonald, whose name appears on the back of countless record albums—from percussion on Carly Simon and James Taylor's "Mockingbird," to writing and playing on "Where Is The Love" which was recorded by Roberta Flack and

Donny Hathaway—with his own debut album "Sound Of A Drum," in 1977, was awarded a Billboard Magazine Disco Award as "Disco Instrumentalist Of The Year." Cissy Houston is another primo session personality who frequently "sits in" on other peoples' releases, including solo vocals on Burt Bacharach albums. She does a great gutsy version of "Tomorrow" (from the Broadway show "Annie") on her own debut album on Private Stock Records. Cissy has two nieces who also sing: Dee Dee Warwick and her sister Dionne Warwick.

Barry also does a rhythm track on "Do You Want To Dance?" and on "Friends," and plays piano on the latter and on "Am I Blue." The production credits were shared by Barry, Geoffrey Haslam, and Ahmet Ertegun, on the following cuts: "Chapel Of Love," "Superstar," "Daytime Hustler," "Leader Of The Pack," "Delta Dawn" and the concluding version of "Friends." On those six songs Miss M's rhythm section is Barry Manilow, piano; Dickie Frank, guitar; Michael Federal, bass; Kevin Ellman, drums. Miss M's choir is Gail Kantor, Merle Miller, and Melissa Manchester who has her own phenomenal songwriting/singing career including "Midnight Blue" and "Come In From The Rain."

What happened next was even more incredible . . . a record deal of his own for Barry! Bette was about to embark on a national tour in the fall/winter of 1973, the same time that Barry's first album, "Barry Manilow I," was released. The tour included thirty-five cities along a four month duration and grossed three million dollars. Before it started, Barry had to first approach Bette's concert promoters with his proposition, "I wouldn't go out on Bette's tour unless they let me do my number!"

he said. And 'they' said, "'Sing in the middle of a Bette Midler act! Are you nuts?'" He may have been 'nuts,' but he got his way, and Barry did his bit at the beginning of the second act of Bette's show, a slot he refers to as "the middle of World War II."

"The first gig I did my number with Bette was in front of 8,000 people in Columbia, Maryland, after she had driven them crazy in the first act. I was sitting at the piano conducting 'Do You Want To Dance?' and I knew, as I finished the last note, with people screaming and yelling as Bette walked off, that after the intermission the first one they were going to see was me. I wasn't on the bill; I was just listed as music director. So nobody knew I was going to come out and sing three of my original songs in the middle of this bedlam. It was outdoors and you could not see the end of the people . . . just thousands of heads. So what did I do? What any other red-blooded American boy would do—I threw up!

"But it worked, I can't figure out why! We played the Red Rock Amphitheater in Colorado, a theater carved right into this mountain, with only the mountain as backdrop. I sang 'Could It Be Magic,' and they went bananas—even with this long Chopin prelude and its being so different from Bette's act. That was my first standing ovation ever."

Concurrent with the tour, the "Barry Manilow" album (the 'I' at the end was added later) sold 35,000 copies. One month before the tour ended in December, 1973 at the Palace Theater on Broadway, Bette's second Atlantic album, "Bette Midler" was released. Also certified "Gold" the release showed further facets of Midler, and paved her way into the Palace Theater.

The album was produced in its entirety by Barry and Arif Mardin. Barry also plays piano throughout and did all of the arranging and conducting. Highlights include: "Drinking Again," "Lullaby of Broadway," "In The Mood," "Uptown," "Da Do Run Run," and "Higher and Higher." Also appearing on this album are Cornell Dupress, guitar; and Stephen Gadd, drums—who are both in the Warner Brothers jazz group that calls themselves Stuff. Ralph MacDonald is again featured on percussion, and contributing to the background vocals is Tasha Thomas. Tasha is the original Auntie Em from the Tony Award-winning Broadway show, "The Wiz," and demonstrated her full pre-tornado velocity on the number from the Grammy Award-winning cast album, "The Feeling We Once Had." The back photo of Miss M's "Bette Midler" L.P. was taken by Manilow's favorite shutterbug, Lee Gurst (who took the photograph for the cover of this book).

The "Bette Midler" L.P. hit the "Top Twenty" that winter. Bette's Broadway show sold out for a solid three-week run, after which Bette went on a year's vacation to recuperate from a case of total exhaustion. She had gone from the Baths on West 74th Street to Broadway's Palace Theater on West 47th Street in the short span of less than two years. Although it was only a matter of twenty-seven blocks, or ironically, an inversion of the two street numbers, she had to cross the country twice, working hard each time she hit the stage. The audience knew that she gave her all and they loved her for it.

In January, 1974 Bette, and her back-up group The Harlettes, and her band including her arranger, conductor, and friend, Barry Manilow

... were all off on their own. Before Bette and Barry's divergence from each other's paths however, during that first month of 1974, it was announced that Bette was mentioned in the 16th Annual Grammy Award Nominations in two categories, for "Best New Artist" and for "Album Of The Year" with "The Divine Miss M." In the case of the later category, both the recording artist and the producers of the album (including Barry) are listed among the nominees.

Competing against Bette in the "Best New Artist" contest were nominees Eumir Deodato, Maureen McGovern, Marie Osmond, and Barry White. The "Album Of The Year" category pitted Charlie Rich's "Behind Closed Doors," Stevie Wonder's "Innervisions," Roberta Flack's "Killing Me Softly With His Song," and Paul Simon's "There Goes Rhymin' Simon" against Bette's "Divine Miss M." Stevie Wonder's "Innervisions" won the prize.

On February 2, 1974 the Grammy Awards was telecast. For the fourth year in a row, Andy Williams was master of ceremonies.

Someone had the inspired idea to have The Carpenters present Bette Midler with the deserved award "Best New Artist." Anyone who knew anything about Bette knew that Karen Carpenter is one of Miss M's favorite insult targets. (In her act she jabs, "Karen Carpenter is so clean you could run your finger down her and she'd squeak!")

Midler quipped on the awards presentation as she gleamed at her statuette, "Isn't this a 'hoot' getting this from 'Miss Karen?' I'm surprised she didn't hit me over the head with this thing!"

It was obvious that Bette was going to win in that category. Her only possible competition was

Maureen McGovern, who was up for the award for her hit "The Morning After."

Stevie Wonder did fantastically well in the nominations, setting a leading record with six nominations in one year, he then went ahead to win four of them, including "Album of the Year." When Stevie took the stage to accept his second Grammy of the evening, defeating Jim Croce's "Bad, Bad Leroy Brown" with his own "You Are The Sunshine Of My Life," he said in a choked-up voice, "I accept this for Jim Croce, a talent man." Wonder's tribute to the late Croce was one of the evening's few serious moments.

Just for the record, Roberta Flack's "Killing Me Softly With His Song" won the award for "Song Of The Year." Bette got one of her awards, and Barry got a taste of the Grammy nominations and awards presentation, and it wouldn't be long before his name was placed on the list as a nominated headlining performer in his own right.

The beginning of 1974 Barry spent assembling his own act. Bette's Harlettes were also out of work, so Barry adopted them for the time being, and readied himself for the road and further promotion on his first album. It wasn't long before more changes came about, and by fall of that year, and the release of "Mandy," Barry was going to not only surprise himself but the entirety of the music-listening public as well!

II
ART ON THE CHARTS:
or . . . Happiness is a Lady Named Mandy

"A lot of people think I left Bette willingly." Barry is quick to clarify. "It wasn't that at all. After the tour, she simply stopped working to take a long rest. There was no choice about it. Looking back though, I guess it was good it happened."

One of the first things that Barry had to do was to decide exactly what it was that he was going to present to his audiences. Prior to his first four-city test tour, Manilow carefully examined his standpoint, at that time, with only his first album recorded.

That spring, prior to setting out on the road, a few close friends of Barry's were invited to Carroll's Rehearsal Studios on West Forty-first Street for a special pre-tour preview of Barry's first headline act. Half a dozen rows of metal chairs were set up in the low-ceilinged room. The "house" went dark, and anticipative electricity charged the air. That first moment, when the spotlight hit the thin, blonde pianist fronting a troupe of four musicians and three back-up girls, history was made. When the applause subsided, Barry gave the greeting that started him on his way: "I invited you to try it all out. I'm glad you came."

On the first tour that spring Barry was quick to pick up on the fact that the crowds who became aware of him were decidedly different from the crowds he had been used to. Although Bette's audience was of legal drinking age; his wasn't necessarily, and he began to make sure of the regulations of the places where he was playing.

Through all of these experiences, Barry was clearly amassing quite a winning team of people behind him, so that his confidence both on stage and off could be based upon his own assurance that all of the details were running smoothly behind him. Three of the heaviest were and are Miles Lourie, his manager; Ron Dante, his co-producer; and a newcomer at this point in Manilow's career, Clive Davis, his record company's president.

An amazing figure in the recording industry, Clive Davis is a born "survivor" with a remarkable story of his own. The president of Arista Records, Davis, like Manilow, is a native of Brooklyn. Having graduated New York University on a full-tuition scholarship, he went on to finish his education at Harvard Law School. Four years past his Harvard graduation he began to work for Columbia Records, and by 1966 was successfully managing that company's domestic activities. In 1967, Davis was officially named president of that company.

Known as a pace-setter, Clive introduced artists such as Janis Joplin and Santana to the listening public. He was responsible for many of the major musical trends of the late sixties and early seventies. Everything seemed to be running smoothly from Davis' office in the CBS headquarters building on West 52nd Street, a monolithic ebony-colored structure known as the "Black Rock."

Everything was cruising along nicely until one particular Tuesday in May, 1973. It was the 29th of the month, the day after Memorial Day when Clive was suddenly fired from Columbia. The official reason for the executive axing was announced by CBS as having to do with Clive misusing some $94,000 in company funds. Cited expenditures were publicized as including renovation of his Manhattan apartment, the rental of a summer house in Beverly Hills, and an extravagant Bar Mitzvah for his son at The Plaza Hotel. However, investigative reports from both *Time* and *Newsweek* tended to point to the fact that by firing Davis, CBS could saddle him with blame for further legal woes. Within the next year, Clive Davis was assessing a new host of offers made open to him.

The opportunity that he did choose to pursue led him to Bell Records. After establishing himself with Bell, he changed the company name and image, and dumped all of its artists; with the exception of three. Barry Manilow and Melissa Manchester were two of the retained. As proof of Clive's business know-how, in the span of less than three years, he had inflated Arista to the sixth largest recording label in the music industry.

Says Clive of the transitory moves that brought him to Bell in the spring of 1974, "Alan Hirschfield approached me with the concept of forming a brand new company with Columbia Pictures whereby I would also have starting energy. Columbia Pictures would make a substantial capital contribution over and above the contribution of whatever I was interested in from their Bell Records artist roster. From the very beginning the concept was to start a new company, and that's what Arista is. It's really not an outgrowth of Bell. We never viewed it that way and I certainly never looked upon it that way. That's why I first came in as a consultant.

"If I was going to come in as head of Bell," Davis explains, "and then later switch to Arista, I would have come in as president of Bell. I didn't come in as president of Bell; I came in as a consultant because I only wanted to study the artist roster for a six-month period of time, see if I felt strongly about any of the artists that existed there and then drop everyone else. So in that six-month period of time I studied the Bell artist roster very carefully and eventually ended up with three artists, namely Melissa Manchester, Barry Manilow, and The Bay City Rollers, for our new company: Arista."

Clive tells of his method of selective criteria that led him to retain Barry's contract along with the other two, "All that we have attempted to establish with premeditation is that Arista means 'quality' and that we are trying to launch artists who have standards. Naturally, that will vary in degrees because one is also looking for commercial success. It would be hypocritical to say you're not. But to establish the identity of the artist is all important. When I was at Columbia, I would always say: 'Snap your fingers and think of Janis Joplin, or Dylan, or Springsteen, or Miles Davis.' You wouldn't think of a company; you would immediately conjure up the personalities of those distinctive artists. That's what I'm continuing to strive for at Arista. It takes a while to build up the personality, the persona, the identification of an artist, but that's the goal.

"So," Davis continues, "when you sign an artist, you judge whether it's all there, but you just can't tell what the pattern of development will be.

Sometimes it doesn't go on from there. You don't know. What I'm thrilled about at Arista is that the artists that have emerged—like Barry Manilow or Melissa Manchester or Patti Smith or Eric Carmen—are each in their own way showing the drive for continued growth that I love to see. They're willing to work hard and push themselves to the limit of their ability."

The album "Barry Manilow II" was produced by Barry and Ron Dante at The Hit Factory and at Media Sound Studios. With four different lyricists, Barry wrote seven of the ten songs that it includes.

Among the other cuts on the album was a Motown classic, written by William Stevenson, Sylvia Moy, and Ivy Hunter, and originally made a hit by Martha Reeves and The Vandellas called, "My Baby Loves Me." Barry's version gives a new melodic interpretation to the lyrics.

Says Martha of her original 1966 version, "'My Baby Loves Me' came at a time when we were trying to get a new sound and I fell in love with it, and it's about my favorite of all my recordings. When I first heard 'My Baby Loves Me' I had had an experience with a boyfriend, and we were about to break up. This one kind of brought all my feelings to home, therefore they were shown on the record, we were about to break up; and this song got us back together. So, in the studio I had a chance to express a feeling inside."

Coincidentally, in the mid-seventies, after Martha Reeves left Motown Records she went on to record a solo debut album on MCA Records with Richard Perry producing, and dissatisfied with their marketing of her album, she next came to Arista Records.

"That's Clive's strategy. He feels that if you have a hit single, then an album's no problem," said Martha.

At that time the Arista L.P. "The Rest Of My Life" was being pieced together with a host of different producers. Although the album yielded no smash singles, it was an interesting excursion for Martha, who is very selective about her material. "You have to consider the lyrics," she insists. "I, as a singer, consider the lyrics to see if I can commit to them, if I can live the part of the writers in writing."

Barry obviously agrees with Martha's taste. In his first Carnegie Hall concert he brought down the house with a Martha and The Vandellas medley!

"Clive showed me 'Mandy'—'Brandy,' as it was called originally," Barry recalls of the Scott English/Richard Kerr composition. "First we changed the name to 'Mandy.' I went into the studio to record it and Clive came down and sat next to the piano. He had his eyes closed and he swayed and moaned and sang along. He's moved to tears at the drop of a hat, Clive. He said, 'Oh, it's wonderful, wonderful! Barry, if you have a hit with this ballad, your career is made.'

The single "Mandy" was released in the fall of 1974, and from the time it came out it began to rise on the charts at a phenomenal pace. In the middle of "Mandy's" ascension came Barry's headlining concert in Carnegie Hall. The November 12, 1974 outing drew rave reviews, and by January, 1975, "Mandy" went to "Number One" on the nation's charts and was certified "Gold."

The "Gold" certification is given by the Record Industry Association of America (R.I.A.A.) for sales of 500,000 units; "Platinum" for sales of

1,000,000 units; and "Double Platinum" for sales of 2,000,000 units. Also in January, 1975, the second single from that album was released, "It's A Miracle." After placing itself in the "Top Ten," it drew Barry further recognition, and he began to have second thoughts about the caliber of some of the cuts on his first album entitled then "Barry Manilow." So, in April he went into Media Sound Studios in New York and re-mixed some of the tracks of the original album, namely, "One Of These Days," "Oh My Lady," "Sweet Life," and "Could It Be Magic." The new version was then re-released as "Barry Manilow I."

In June, his next single was released, but according to Barry, he felt the song was a long-shot gamble as a hit.

While "Could It Be Magic?" was busily on its way to "Gold" status, Barry was back in the studio, working on his third album, "Tryin' To Get The Feeling." Recorded during the summer of 1975, it was released that October, was certified "Gold" four weeks after it's release, and, like "Barry Manilow I," eventually went "Platinum."

The third album marked a further development in Barry's musical scope and offered a fuller refinement of his sound. Barry's band at this point consisted of Alan Axelrod, keyboards; Sid McGinnis, guitar; Steve Donaghey, bass; and Lee Gurst, drums and percussion. Also, his back-up trio, which later evolved into Lady Flash, was at this point billed as The Flashy Ladies, and included Debra Byrd, Ramona Brooks, and Reperata (Lorraine Mazzola).

Among the selections are Bruce Johnston's "I Write The Songs," Larry Wess' "Lay Me Down," and Phil Galdston and Peter Thom's "Why Don't

We Live Together." The later pair of composers were the 1975 Grand Prize winners in The American Song Festival contest. Later, the recognition that Barry brought to them by recording this song led to their own Warner Brothers recording contract, and they now perform under the name Galdston and Thom.

The title cut, "Tryin' To Get The Feeling Again," was penned by a singer/songwriter by the name of David Pomeranz. On his Arista album "It's In Everyone Of Us" is a completely different version of "Tryin'. . ."—the one that Manilow made famous—and is well worth checking out.

It begins: "At any moment/She'll be walkin' through that door/But she won't find me behind it. 'Cause the feeling is gone and/It just won't come back anymore," and includes quite a few other stanzas missing from the Manilow version. Back-up singers on the Pomeranz album include Gary ("Dream Weaver") Wright, Alan ("Undercover Angel") O'Day, and Melissa Manchester.

Another of Barry's entrys on L.P. number three is "Bandstand Boogie" which is in actuality the original "American Bandstand" theme from the Dick Clark TV show. The music was composed by a quartet of instrumentalists including Les and Larry Elgart, who are both icons of the 1940's "swing" sound. For the first time in the song's history, Barry Manilow and Bruce Sussman have given it its own lyrics. One particular stanza spotlights the show's ageless star, "Hey it's Mr. Dick Clark/What a place you've got here/Swell spot the music's hot here/Best in the East/give it at least a seventy five!"

Barry's music fills the rest of the album. In partnership with Enoch Anderson are "She's A

Star" and "A Nice Boy Like Me;" with Marty Panzer, "New York City Rhythm;" and with Adrienne Anderson, "As Sure As I'm Standin' Here."

During the fall of 1975, Barry was amid a three-month tour which included an engagement with Helen Reddy headlining at the MGM Grand Hotel. The date was Manilow's Las Vegas debut. The tour ended New Year's Eve, 1975, at The Beacon Theater in New York City.

In a press release dated December 22, 1975, it was announced that Barry's Beacon Theater performance was being given for the benefit of the disadvantaged, as his Christmas present to New York. The release furthered, "Recording star, Barry Manilow, will conclude his outstandingly successful three-month fall tour with a special free concert on New Year's Eve afternoon at New York's Beacon Theater at 3:00 p.m. The performance is being given in association with Hospital Audience Inc. (H.A.I.), who has arranged for 2000 institutionalized and disadvantaged individuals from orphanages, drug programs, schools for the emotionally disturbed and retarded, and senior citizen centers and homes to attend. The free show is for these invited guests and is not open to the public."

At a press conference held that day at noon, Barry said, "I've always wanted to do a free concert. This year has been fantastic to me and since my success has come from pop-AM radio I figured the audience who would get off most on what I do would be an AM audience, older folks and kids."

The single "I Write The Songs" was released at the same time as the "Tryin' To Get The Feeling Again" album, in October of 1975. By January

1976 the song was "Number One" on the charts, and certified "Gold." The crazy thing about the song was the fact that although the entire country was listening to the record, quite a few people completely missed the essence of the lyrics.

"It has been strange lately," Barry noted. "People come up to me and say, 'How can you live with yourself by singing "I am Music and I write the songs"?' I say, 'Wait a minute, I'm not saying I am Music . . . I'm playing a character in that song: Music, all the music all those years!' But I nearly made a call to Bruce Johnston, a real pro who wrote the song and said, 'Maybe we should sing "It is Music, that writes the songs."'" I just read in the music column in the Sunday News, 'On The Record,' a question posed to disc jockeys: 'What do you think of today's lyrics?' One D.J. answered that he thinks lyricists of the sixties are making comebacks with really good lyrics: Paul Simon and Bob Dylan, and I agree. I really respect and admire Paul Simon—integrity. He has got such class.

"Then this disc jockey says that 'Some pop artists today are writing real trash like "I Write The Songs." Who wants to hear a guy singing that he writes every song ever written?' I thought, 'Oh, no, man!' A disc jockey, he's playin' the song every day and he still hasn't figured out what it means! Then it dawns on me that this song has sold close to two million records, and it has been 'Number One' on the charts. If everyone who heard it thought I was on this ego trip, they wouldn't have bought it!"

As the old year of 1975 ended, Barry had amassed the following honorary distinctions:

—Over 4,000,000 Singles Sold in 1975
—Over 1,600,000 Albums Sold in 1975

—#1—Top New Male Vocalist/Singles
   —*Record World*
   —*Cashbox*
—#1—Top New Male Vocalist/Albums
   —*Record World*
   —*Cashbox*
—#1—Top New Male Artist/*Music Retailer*
—#1—Pop Artist Of The Year/*Radio & Records*

The week of January 24, 1976 was when the music industry's trade publications ran The National Academy of Recording Arts and Sciences (N.A.R.A.S.) nominations of entrants to receive Grammy Awards in forty-eight categories for the previous year's accomplishments. Barry's "Mandy" was on the list in the category of "Record of the Year" nominees. Competing against it were Janis Ian's "At Seventeen," The Eagles' "Lyin' Eyes," The Captain and Tennille's "Love Will Keep Us Together," and Glen Campbell's "Rhinestone Cowboy."

On February 28, 1976, the 18th Annual Grammy Awards presentation was telecast live from The Hollywood Paladium. As Joan Baez handed Stevie Wonder the "Record Of The Year" winning envelope, Barry was sitting nervously in his seat in the audience. Reading in braille, Stevie announced that the Captain and Tennille had won the award.

"The Grammy this year?" Barry said afterwards. "They should have photographed my legs shaking. That audience—it was like performing at Sam Goody's. I was looking out at all the album covers I'd ever seen in my life. If 'Mandy' had won, it would have been a surprise to me. 'Love Will

Keep Us Together' was in fact the biggest record of the year."

That spring *After Dark Magazine* presented Barry with their annual Ruby Award as their "Performer Of The Year." The gala affair held for the awards took place at the Starlight Roof of the Waldorf-Astoria. Clive Davis presented Manilow with a "Platinum" record to signify his million-selling album "Tryin' To Get The Feeling Again." Among the guests were Shirley MacLaine, Lady Flash, Nona Hendryx of Labelle, Linda Allen, Miles Lourie, Ron Dante, and others.

Barry knew Melissa Manchester from Brooklyn, and at many different points in their careers their paths have crossed. When Bette Midler was starting out, Melissa at one point was one of her Harlettes, but soon, like Manilow, made her own emergence out of the background and on up front to the footlights. In September, 1975, at The Schaffer Music Festival in Central Park, Barry and Melissa, both with their own solo identities, teamed up for a two-set show. First Melissa did her set, a brief intermission, Barry's set, and then the two of them did a duo finale. In January, 1976, simultaneous with the announcement of Barry's accumulated 1975 laurels, Melissa had amassed many distinctions of her own including: #1—Top New Female Vocalist/Albums *(Cashbox);* #1—Top New Female Vocalist/singles *(Cashbox);* #1—Top New Female Artist *(Music Retailer);* #1—Top Easy Listening Singles Award/"Midnight Blue" *(Billboard).*

Says Melissa of her own identity establishment, "When I first went solo, there was a tremendous amount of comparison, and interviews were mainly about Bette, which was very difficult to handle on any level. The direction the interviewers were trying to get into was: scoop! I don't like that. But that was just in the beginning, and it was understandable. It's always easier for people to compare you to someone else than to try to find something authentic or original. I am quite sure that there were lots of traits left over—it's difficult not to have them, but then, hopefully, after the years, you come into your own."

Lyricist Carole Bayer Sager, who now has her own album on Electra, first saw Melissa when she was singing behind Bette in Carnegie Hall and got in contact with her. Composing collaborations between Carole and Melissa have included "Midnight Blue" and "Come In From The Rain."

According to Melissa, "What happens when we write is that we talk a lot, and that's usually how ideas come. I would imagine that we were both going through something that was indirectly related to the song." She explains about "Midnight Blue": "It sounded like a nice song, you know? I was kind of surprised at the reaction of that song . . . but then I wasn't. After a while, when you get to know the business of music, you're surprised by strange things, and not surprised by most things!

"Working with Bette was fabulous," she reflects. Then on the success of Manilow she looks into her not-so-distant memories to point out that, "For Barry, it's more than we ever thought on those cold, depressing nights."

After the Grammy's in 1976, Barry's next couple of projects were released to the public in a steady flow. In March, the single "Tryin' To Get The Feeling" came out, and by May was in the "Top Ten." The Lady Flash debut album on RSO Records, "Beauties In The Night," was released that summer along with the single "Street Singin'," which effortlessly parlayed itself into the late summer "Top Forty." By this time the trio had evolved into the present triad of Debra Byrd, Monica Burruss, and Reparata (formerly of Reparata and The Delrons). Produced by Barry and Ron Dante at Media Sound Studios, Manilow wrote half of the tunes with aid from his usual bank of lyricists.

In July of the bicentennial year, Arista Records released Barry's fourth album, "This One's For You." So incredible was the immediate demand for the disc that it was "Shipped Gold," in other words there were already orders for the first 500,000 copies of the album before they left the pressing plant. Within a short time it had become Barry's third "Platinum" L.P.

That November, the single version of "This One's For You" was strongly lodged in the "Top Twenty," two months after its release, and its successor, "Weekend In New England," began its charted rise.

Early in the year Barry had projected the contents of his fourth album, titled after his composition with Marty Panzer, "This One's For You."

"In my next album I may move on, too," he had previewed of changing trends, " . . . do a whole instrumental thing. This fourth album is all my own material. It's a really nice pop album, a step further than the last one. But you never know. I always love the struggle that comes with changing."

That statement was made in early spring, and by the time the album did come out, it contained nine Barry Manilow originals, and an additional two cuts were the hit singles, "Weekend In New England" and "Looks Like We Made It." The latter was written by Richard Kerr and Will Jennings, and the former was penned by Randy Edelman.

The original version of "Weekend In New England" is contained on a 1975 release on 20th Century Records, Randy Edelman's "Farewell Fairbanks" album. In addition to his showcased compositions is a great version of "Concrete and Clay" and musical contributions by Jackie DeShannon, Nigel Olsson, Dee Murphy, Andrew Gold, and Melissa Manchester.

Of the composition that Barry Manilow made famous, Edelman tells this story, "I was in England," he recalls, "doing TV shows because a record of mine had broken over there. One night, after a show, I got back to my hotel and there was a note saying Clive Davis had called. I thought it was a joke, right? I mean I couldn't get Clive Davis on the phone here! He was saying how much he liked 'Weekend In New England' and how he was going to give it to Barry Manilow.

He phoned Davis and the next thing he knew was that Davis "was off on a detailed discussion of why the harmonics in the verse didn't work. I really couldn't believe it. I mean, most record company presidents don't even know what's on their albums even after they're out, and here's Clive Davis giving me suggestions about how to rewrite a song when the guy who's going to record it hasn't even heard it yet. He did it in a way that I didn't feel that my creativity was being challenged. He told me I could tell him to bug off if I felt like it, and that he'd give the song to Barry anyway. It was just that he thought some simplification could really make it a hit. And he was right."

All of the parties involved obviously made the

proper impressions on each other. Randy rewrote some of the song. Clive gave Barry the song. Barry recorded the song and made it a hit. And, as if that's not a happy enough ending to the tale, Clive offered Randy a record deal, and Edelman is now under contract to Arista!

On Barry's "This One's For You" album, Lady Flash handled the background vocals, Manilow played piano and sang, Steven Donaghey played bass, Alan Axelrod did additional keyboards, and the drums were played by Lee Gurst. Lee is also responsible for the front and back album cover photos on this album, as well as the back cover shot of Barry and his beagle, Bagel, on the "Tryin' To Get The Feeling Again" album.

Along with the album releases and upward-shooting singles, Barry, his band, and his back-up group hit the road at the end of July for what was a scheduled 98-city nation-wide concert tour. The ticket sales were completely phenomenal. From three of the first eight scheduled engagements came these responses:

Our first date sold out within hours and we still have enough requests for two or three additional days.
—MEADOWBROOK   FESTIVAL, Rochester, Michigan

Fans waited overnight to purchase tickets for an added day and did so in two hours!
—RAVINIA FESTIVAL, Chicago

Barry Manilow is the hottest ticket of the season.
—UNIVERSAL AMPHITHEATRE, Los Angeles

About the same time that the fourth album was released, and the tour was announced, it was also disclosed that the following March would be the broadcast of the first Barry Manilow TV special.

The 98-city concert tour which began July 31, 1976, was set to extend to April 13, 1977, and would include some very important milestone performances in Barry's still-growing career. Not only would it include his first Broadway headlining engagement December to January, but his debut Nevada casino headlining, too.

Having returned from the road prior to his Broadway opening curtain, Barry admitted that he had been forewarned of the perils of selling tickets to such an event. Their thoughts were well-intended, but to the surprise of all, the entire run of the show from December 21, 1976 to January 2, 1977 sold-out the 1,900 seat Uris Theater every night!

In January, 1977, the Grammy Awards nominations were announced for those songs that were on the music charts from October 15, 1975 to October 15, 1976. In the top category were nominated songs and performers, "Afternoon Delight" by The Starland Vocal Band, "50 Ways To Leave Your Lover" by Paul Simon, "If You Leave Me Now" by Chicago, "This Masquerade" by George Benson, and "I Write The Songs" by Barry, all vying for the title of "Record Of The Year."

Spurned by Barry's hit single version of it, former Beach Boy Bruce Johnston was nominated for "Song Of The Year" for his penning of "I Write The Songs." Pitted against Bruce were songwriters and works, Bill Danoff for "Afternoon Delight," Neil Sedaka and Howard Greenfield for "Breaking Up Is Hard To Do," Leon Russell for

"This Masquerade," and Gordon Lightfoot for "Wreck Of The Edmond Fitzgerald."

On February 19, 1977 the awards presentation was broadcast "live" internationally. Among the performed nominated songs was a very good segment of Manilow doing "I Write The Songs" for a world-wide simultaneous audience, via satellite.

George Benson, the master musician who this year has popularized his jazz guitaring for the mass listening audience to get into, won a total of four well-deserved awards out of seven nominations, including, "Record Of The Year" for the song, "This Masquerade," while the L.P. "Breezin'" picked up engineering and pop instrumental honors. Stevie and his wonderous "Songs In The Key Of Life" grabbed him best album, producer, and pop male performer Grammy. The song "I Wish" gave Stevie a tie with Benson at four wins out of eight in the "net that statuette" competition.

As Bette Midler best summed up the proceedings: "Los Angeles: Home of nothing . . . but the record business; where you're only as good as your last two minutes and forty-two seconds!"

Unfortunately, Barry for the second year in a row was among the nominees but failed to win in the final tally. On the bright side, Bruce Johnston was honored with the "Song Of The Year" award for "I Write The Songs." Barry's solo spotlight looked great on the show, and with all that he was into that month, it only added to his 1977 multi-media emergence. Purveying a sleek new look, Manilow came off very *bon vivant* in his dark, wide silk-lapeled, sequined tux coat; black butterfly bow tie; and bib-cut black vest.

The week of February 26, 1977, Barry's single version of "Weekend In New England" was in the

'Top Ten,' and on March 2, the first "Barry Manilow" TV special was broadcast on ABC-TV. The show was aired on a Wednesday evening at 10:00 p.m., and in the Nielsen Ratings the show pulled 35 million viewers, topping the other network shows in that same time slot. Appearing at that same time was a "Dean Martin Special" on NBC and a special drama called "Minstrel Man" on CBS. The one-hour variety special mainly featured Barry's music, and his guests were Lady Flash and Penny Marshall of the TV series "Laverne and Shirley."

Show business weekly publication *Variety* ran a review of "The Barry Manilow Special," which read in part, "Rock recording stars moving over to TV special productions are all faced with the same bugaboo; the style, discipline, the focus and the audience for TV presentation is almost diametrically opposite that required for rock concert success. As a result, few make the transition work.

"Barry Manilow, the latest to try did better than most, primarily because his choice of material and his basic musicianship is better and more sophisticated than most of his peers in the pop music field." That obviously is part of the key to Barry's wide-spread musical appeal.

As a direct result of his television exposure, the week of March 19, 1977 "Barry Manilow I" re-entered the "Billboard" charts, and "Barry Manilow II" had done the same the week previous. This made for the unique occurrence of having four charted albums at one time.

Later that month came Barry's first headlining Nevada casino dates. From March 25 to March 27 he was at the Sahara Tahoe, and from March 31 to April 13 was appearing in Las Vegas at the MGM

Grand Hotel. After that last date, the publicized 98-city tour came to an end, and as had Bette Midler three years previous, Barry and all of his back-up performers professionally parted ways. Manilow took off for Los Angeles for the majority of the summer, where he spent time working on his fifth studio-produced album, and started planning his second television special. At that time Lady Flash as well headed west to plan their second album.

Released at the end of April, by the first week in May, 1977, the single "Looks Like We Made It" from the studio-produced album "This One's For You" entered the record charts with a "bullet" at #88 in Billboard. Also, at the end of that month, the deluxe double-album set, "Barry Manilow Live," was released, and entered Billboard with a "bullet" at #10 in that magazine's "Top 200" album listings the week of May 28. The chart action of these recordings was very significant for many reasons, and Barry's incredibly charismatic sound and vocal identity took them both all the way to the top of the stack!

Barry's fifth album includes "live" versions of all of his hit singles up to and including "Looks Like We Made It," as well as the first recorded version of his "Very Strange Medley," Rupert Holmes "Studio Musician," and a new Barry Manilow/Marty Panzer song called "It's Just Another New Year's Eve." Manilow explains about the song: "All during the two weeks that we were preparing for the New Year's Eve show, I was thinking to myself, 'What can I do for these people who come to see me on New Year's Eve other than just dropping balloons and passing out champagne . . . you know! And, you know its more depressing than it is happy, everybody is like 'Oh no not a new year ... another year! What am I going to do tonight?' I really don't know anyone who really looks forward to that one night. So, I wrote a little tune ... me and Marty sat down and wrote this tune with that in mind. And, this one's for our generation you know ... because I don't know what "Auld Lang Syne" means anyway! What does that mean? So, this one's for 'us.'"

From May 28 to July 16, all five of Barry's existing albums were on the charts together in Billboard for a duration of eight weeks. The week of July 16 "Barry Manilow Live" was Billboard's "Number One" album, and it was denoted that the two-record set had been certified "Platinum;" Barry's fourth! The next week "Looks Like We Made It" became Barry's third "Number One" single, joining "Mandy" and "I Write The Songs" on his growing list.

From the time that "Barry Manilow Live" entered the charts, the week of May 28, and on into that fall, a Warner Brother's release, Fleetwood Mac's "Rumours" literally dominated the "Number One" slot on Billboard's album charts. A phenomenally successful album commercially, artistically, and sales-wise, "Rumours" shattered many previous records set by rock artists. The album sold in excess of the "Quadruple Platinum" mark of four million copies, and the week of August 27, celebrated its sixteenth week at the top of the charts, breaking the previous record set by Peter Frampton's "Frampton Comes Alive" the previous year (which was the first L.P. to shatter the then all-time record set in the early seventies by Carole King's "Tapestry").

"Rumours" commemorates the group's tenth

anniversary and is the second album by the Fleetwood Mac personnel line-up of Mick Fleetwood, Christine McVie, Stevie Nicks, Lindsey Buckingham and John McVie, and was released in early 1977. "Rumours" contains eleven selections of original composition by the members of the band, and each cut represents a different side of the inter-relations of the quintet, romantically, and as friends.

For the entirety of the summer of 1977, the only album on the Billboard charts to interrupt "Rumours" at any point of its seasonal domination of the crowning position of "Number One" was "Barry Manilow Live"! That rumor-breaking feat alone is quite an accomplishment!

As Barry best explains of the contents of the "live" L.P., "These discs were recorded live at the Uris Theater in New York City in December, 1976 while in the middle of a 98-city American tour that began in July, 1976 and ended in April, 1977. We have tried to capture some of the incredible excitement with which we were greeted during those ten months, but it was absolutely impossible to even try to capture other equally incredible moments. That show in Chicago when I took off my jacket with a flourish and my fly was open; that night in Ohio when I ripped Reparata's cape off and it caught on her choker (darn near threw her into the drums before I realized the cape was caught!!), the show when the harp player wouldn't stop playing the last run on 'Weekend in New England' and kept playing all the while I was introducing the next song; that night in Philly when that very strange gentleman jumped up on stage and insisted that he do his imitation of a frog for the entire audience (and he did!!!!).

"Hysterically funny moments and infuriatingly maddening moments; the lousy hotels and the spectacular ones, the planes that were late, the food that was gross, the colds, the flu, the broken bones and all the show business cliches you've ever heard of. But miraculously we have all lived to tell the tale and hopefully some of the miracle is on these records," says Barry optimistically. Whether or not some of the "miracle" made its way onto the grooves or not, isn't half as evident as the 'magic' that did.

III
A MORNING WITH MANILOW:
Barry at Home

It was a gray and overcast Manhattan morning the Thursday I showed up at Barry Manilow's apartment for a scheduled 11:00 a.m. interview. Already the omens of the new day were looking decidedly cloudy; the sky hung gloomily over the city, and my scheduled photographer called at the last minute to tell me that something had come up and she'd never make it to Barry's in time to take pictures.

I felt semi-frantic when I arrived at the modern high-rise apartment building on East 27th Street. What was I going to do for photos for the feature story I was writing on Barry? ... use publicity stills? ... get some concert shots? As I knocked on Manilow's door I told myself that I'd live without exclusive pictures. Although outside it looked like it was about to rain at any moment, once inside and introduced I realized that despite the clouded start, the day was not without its silver lining.

It was September 11, 1975, the day after Barry completed his third album, and the day before he played the concert in Central Park with Melissa Manchester. "Could It Be Magic" had just become his third hit single, and outside of a musically aware audience, the mention of Manilow still drew an occasional "Barry who?"

"People are just beginning to pronounce my

name right!" Barry said, astonished at his snow-balling identity. "Nobody knew I existed until last October—that's when 'Mandy' came out."

In the study of the high-floor terraced midtown apartment he lived in at the time, Barry sat in a high-backed arm-chair, and in a very relaxed but concise fashion, answered my inquiries. I apologized for my photographer's absence. Pointing to the auburn/blonde layered locks that flowed over the back collar of his dress shirt, he said, "And I just washed my hair!"

I sat on a couch next to Barry's chair, and glanced across the room to a video cassette deck and a bookshelf filled with tapes which Barry explained were of his televised appearances.

"Tell me about your new album," I began my line of questioning, as Barry's houseboy brought in two mugs of coffee with cinnamon, and having served them, disappeared.

"O.K., so where were we?" Barry asked taking a sip of his coffee. "Talking about the new album."

Looking downward at the beagle's nose that was resting on my leg, I wanted to make sure that all formal introductions were out of the way and asked, "What's your dog's name?" (I didn't want to address her improperly!)

"This is Bagel my beagle," said Manilow about the new-found furry friend sitting on my right.

"Hello, Bagel beagle!" I greeted. "All right . . ." I began, returning my attention to Barry. At the loss of my attentiveness Bagel stood up and walked across my lap to her master in the chair in the corner.

"Crawl right over!" Barry encouraged the beagle standing on my legs, at which she shifted laps.

"Anyway . . ." I started once again while Bagel

got comfortable, "tell me about your new album."

"It's great! It's terrific!" Manilow glowed. "It took a long time to make, and it's better than the other two. It's not that big a change though. I like the material on the other two; it's good material. It's better production and better singing, and we worked real hard on this one, to make sure that this was going to be a hit, because there's a lot of people that are just becoming acquainted with what I do, so if the first album they buy is this one, I want to make sure that they are happy with it. I mean the solid fans; the people that like what I do, will probably just love this one. I'm really after the people who just have no idea what I do."

As Barry attempted to take a sip of coffee, Bagel decided to wildly scratch her ear, and suddenly looked like she was about to shake her head and douse her master with hot coffee. "I think I'm in trouble if you shake!" he warned his canine friend. "It's ballads and a lot of big productions, and I just love it!" he tried to return to the conversation, but sensing that he was going to be covered with hot coffee, pointed to his clean pressed dress shirt, which was open at the top. A gold chain with a five-pointed star hung close to his throat. "Mind if I sit in my tee shirt?" he asked, not wanting to worry about coffee stains.

"No," I approved amiably. "Feel right at home!"

"Thanks anyway!" Barry laughed at my playing host in his apartment.

"New compositions?" I inquired of the L.P.

Hanging up his shirt on the back of a chair, he resumed talking about the third album which had just been taped. "Yes, either I've written them, or I've found them from other writers, because I don't mind doing other writers' material, because there is so much good stuff out there that I can't just say, 'No, I want to be a singer/songwriter.' If I don't do them, nobody else does. Nobody else does anybody's material anymore, and these guys are running around with good songs ... so there's no reason why I shouldn't do them. There's six that I wrote, and about four or five that I didn't write, and they're nice ... they're just great songs!

"They're putting together the cover now, and putting the credits; the album credits and labels and all of that stuff together. It takes about four weeks to do all of the art work, basically it will be out the beginning of October."

Barry explains that the album has been recorded along with intermittent touring over the last three months. "I've been touring while I've been doing it too. I actually took off about two months to do the album, but it stretched into the beginning of this tour, and I've been coming back and forth to do it, but it's worth it ... it's worth it. Finally we sat down last night after we finished the last song, and we listened to the whole thing in sequence, and it's good! I'll stand behind this one. So, it's good. I have no complaints."

In answer to my questioning the re-mixing of "Barry Manilow I" he commented, "Yes, I had a chance to say, 'If I could have done it again, I would have done this.'"

With all of his running back and forth to New York to finish the album, I wondered if a part of the cycle included doing his writing on the road. "No," he said flatly, "I can't do it on the road, 'cause that stage show just takes the whole concentration. It's the whole thing on the stage show, and that's a lot of running around. We don't settle down in a town for a week or two . . . not anymore. We used to play clubs. When I was doing that we would play two weeks in a club. When we'd get a club, there might have been an opportunity to do that, but even then it was hard. Now it's impossible, I go to Kansas one day, to Maui the next, so it's real hard.

"Anyway, there's no piano! There is never any piano in the room, so I do it all here. When I decide to make another album, I sit down, for a couple of weeks and I start writing it."

"Anybody notable whose compositions you're using?" I asked.

"No, I don't think so." Barry thought for a second. "I mean, they're terrific writers, but none of them really have . . . notoriety."

"Not yet . . ." I laughed, ". . . not til the album comes out!"

"Not yet," he replied. "Well, I don't know what I do for them. I don't know if I put Scott English on the map, even though he wrote 'Mandy,' I don't think anyone even knows Scott, and people keep asking who wrote that one. And no one faints when I say that."

On "Barry Manilow I" and "Barry Manilow II" Barry tackled two songs with Jon Hendricks lyrics, on which he did all thirty-two separate vocal tracks. Since it looked like a solid pattern, and since good things usually come in threes, I asked him if there was to be another similar selection on the third L.P. to match "Cloudburst" and "Avenue C" respectively on the first two. What I discovered from Barry was the fact that the technique would be repeated on a familiar tune with new lyrics, not by Hendricks, but by Manilow and Sussman.

"I did one," he verified my hunch, "I always do one on an album. I love to do that kind of thing, so I put special lyrics to the old 'American Bandstand Theme.' It never had lyrics, I researched it and I found out that there were never any lyrics put to it, so I sat down with a friend of mine, Bruce Sussman. He's a fabulous lyricist, and both of us started, just as a kick; we started writing lyrics to it. I called Dick Clark and he sent me the original version of the 'Bandstand Theme' that I heard when I was growing up, because what I hear now has got a moog synthesizer on it, and not the old 'Big Band' theme. So I copied the old 'Big Band' thing. We put lyrics to it, note for note, even the old saxophone solo; we put lyrics to that part too. And I did my little thirty-two voices on it, and it's really fun! It came out great!"

"It's just an over-dub," Barry explained of how one vocalist is able to do thirty-two tracks in rhythmic sync. "The tape is big, and it's divided into sixteen different tracks. You record one on top of the other, and as you record, then you play back what you record and harmonize to it. Then you play back both of those, and harmonize to that . . . and then you just keep playing it. That's why it says thirty-two vocals, which means there's thirty-two separate vocals, but I'm harmonizing to most of them. It's not like I was singing the same thing. It's all harmonies, and all background stuff."

On Barry's living room wall, next to certified "Gold" copies of "Mandy" and the album "Barry Manilow II" are framed "Gold" editions of Bette's L.P.'s "The Divine Miss M" and "Bette Midler" which Barry received for his co-production duties on both. I inquired as to their friendship and the possibility of their working together again in any capacity?

"No," he said bluntly to anything on record. "She was over yesterday. But, I haven't had time. She's been in the studio for like three months. It takes her quite a long time to do an album, because she's a stickler for what she wants, and it has to be perfect . . . or at least perfect to her. It might be perfect to everybody else, and she's not happy with it. So it takes her much longer than it would me. I think basically because I'm a musician I can probably get what I want easier than Bette can, because she can't play an instrument. You know, she has to communicate it to an entire bunch of people. Whereas I can sit down and play what I want, and maybe communicate it easier to my musicians, it takes her a little longer to try to get that to them. So . . . it takes *her* a little longer. I heard a ballad that she had done . . . it's fabulous! Just fabulous! If the rest of the album's like that she'll be great!

"I'm really not working for her anymore. I'm her friend, you know . . . we hang out together, but I'm really not involved in that part of her life anymore."

In our conversation Barry mentioned having done production work with Sally Kellerman, but as far as Midler, "For Bette? Not for Bette. Eventually I'm sure we'll get back together again. I mean . . . there's just no time, frankly I'd love to go back and get it out for her; to go back on the road with her would be a lot of laughs. But, there's just no time. Me thinking about going out together, man that's just crazy, it's too soon."

"The first time I saw you," I said to Barry, "was at the Masonic Temple in Detroit."

"In Detroit?" Barry flashed back to Detroit, "Was I doing a little singing over there?"

Having gotten an affirmative answer, he continued with a smile, "Oh, that worked out great! We had a great time doing that, but it's too soon for me to go out with Bette as a duet. There's not enough people who know what I do and she still wants to do it by herself . . . anyway . . . so, maybe. Maybe; I don't know, in a couple of years we'll wind up with Bette and Barry." Making the shape of a heart with his fingers in the air over Bagel's head, "In a little heart, they get in the middle of a boxing ring . . . a tasteful boxing ring!" he laughed.

When I asked him how he made his emergence from behind the piano and onto the forestage, he exclaimed, "I was thrown from behind the piano! Because, at the time Arista was Bell Records, and they wouldn't give me a record deal, unless I promised I would go out and perform, and I didn't really want to go out and perform, but I did want to make records. Because, I really loved being in the studio. So, I put an act together, you know I think I know how to do that . . . I've been doing that for about ten years, and coaching people. So, it was easy enough to put that together. I made sure that part was solid, because I had never performed, and I figured if I fainted on the stage nobody should know it! The act would be so good, so strong that nobody would realize that I was just dying up there if it happened.

"So, we put it together, and it came out real strong, and it gave me a foundation to be able to make mistakes as a performer, because the basis was so strong, the music and the girls singing and the band. Even if I did get lost in it, the act would still look powerful. I didn't want to give the whole burden to me, because I'd never done it before, and yet here I was headlining in Philadelphia, and headlining all over the place. I had never done it before. Little by little, I got into it. Now I really enjoy it; I really enjoy performing! It's fun, basically I enjoy making music, but I wouldn't put a lampshade on my head just to get attention. I like the music, and I like *making* the music, and I like the audience reacting; because I'm doing it for them! So, it's a nice trip!" he said with elation of his progress on stage from pianist to performer.

After asking about The Harlettes, I received this chronology from Barry: "I had them for my first tour because they were out of work, and I knew them, and they still knew my material. So, I took them along with me, but when I came back from my first six months on the road, I decided I would get my own girls, because it wasn't my girls. It was Bette's Harlettes. So, I figured as long as I had decided on that type of group for Bette, I decided on that type of group for me because they sound best behind me. So, I hired three different girls, and it's good! I love The Harlettes they are all my friends, and they went back to work for Bette, and everybody's happy now!"

Manilow continued on the subject of Clive and Arista: "They just changed the name, Clive Davis came in and decided to change the name from Bell to Arista. It was just a title change. My contract is still the same, and Clive became president of the company. And, I think he gave the company a different look. Because Bell Records really had the feel of a singles record company; more of a Tony Orlando and Dawn singles record company. Clive is giving it some class, because he's a classy man."

When I asked what the third album was to be

titled, Barry informed me that he had just decided, after listening to the entire album the night before, conclusively upon the title cut, "Tryin' To Get The Feeling."

"It's a title of one of the songs on the album, and it's evidently a pretty hot song. So, we're going to call it 'Tryin' To Get The Feeling.'"

As far as pre-release single potential for the title cut, he pondered for a second, then admitted that after listening to the complete master, he was unsure. "I don't know, it's a nice title no matter what. Whether it's a single or not? It's a nice title . . . it's possibly a single, but there's others too."

On the subject of single releases, I probed, "How much control do you have over what is released as a single?"

"Oh, I confer with Clive and Ronny," he explained, "and we all make a decision jointly, but most of the time there really isn't really any decision, it's just obvious which one it is. I wish there was a big decision, it's just obvious which one it is. I wish there was a big decision, I mean with about five different single records; and we don't know which one to pick . . . I'd be very happy about that. The problem comes when there are no singles on the album, and you don't want to release any of them! But, so far we've been lucky. We didn't know whether we'd want to release 'Miracle' first or 'Mandy' first, or maybe even 'Early Morning Stranger,' or any of the other ones on that second album. There were a whole bunch of them, that given the right attention, and the right push, could have become successful, you know.

"I think the same thing goes for this one. Although, when I'm in the middle of making an album I don't know, I hear it thirty-five times a night, so don't ask me! When they told me that's a good one, I said, 'Fine.' I don't know, it was just another song at that point, and I had heard it five thousand times. So, I really have to rely on Clive in that he shows it to people that don't know what I do, or he shows it to people that are very into the record industry and that have had all the experience. And if everybody reacts unanimously on one particular song, then it's obvious that's the one to release. I don't care which one they release myself . . . I love 'em all! If they work, I'll be very happy with it."

With "Could It Be Magic?" being a hit after the "Barry Manilow" album was re-mixed into "Barry Manilow I," I wondered if there had been any previous singles culled from it? Explained my host, "'Sweetwater Jones,' that was the single release. It got picked up in Philadelphia, but it's hard. I had never done anything; they couldn't even pronounce my name, why should they play the record!? You know; so it never really happened, but it was strange. On the first album we had sold like 35,000 copies of my first album, and it was sold on the basis of 'Could It Be Magic?' Everybody kept showing it to their friends on the basis of 'Could It Be Magic?' and then the second album came out, and . . . 'Mandy,' and 'Miracle,' and Clive heard 'Magic' and said, 'You know, you should have done something with that!' But, it was a seven-minute cut! What are you . . . I mean, they (the radio stations) wouldn't play 'Sweetwater Jones!' What made you think they were going to play a seven-minute cut? From a *Chopin Prelude!* And, he said, 'I think it's time to try it now, you can't lose anything . . . because if it doesn't make it, nobody will know that we released it. Because, there'll be a third album coming out right away!'

"So, we tried it, and it worked! I can't believe it! It sounds so ridiculous in the middle of all that Kung Fu Fighting stuff. It's great! I'm so happy it's being played. That was a hard one, I mean they had to pull teeth to get that one on the air. It was the public that did it, because the radio stations didn't want to play it. I mean it was just not their kind of song. It was nice, beautiful, but why waste five-minutes on a ballad. When they finally gave in and went on with it, the phones just lit up! The people would just call in, and they would change their minds and keep playing it. But it was just like pulling teeth to get them to play that record. Yes, I'm real proud of that one!"

Since his recording of the new album was already completed, I asked him about his upcoming plans.

"Well, I'm going back on the road," Manilow replied. "I'm basically on the road right now. I'm back and forth into the city. So, my head is into performing now, now I'm just continually on the phone. My band, my girls are rehearsing, we're figuring out what to do next. After that I guess I'll make another album, but I don't know. I've got to stop for a while. I've been doing it for a while, I've got to take some time off. I don't know, I was thinking of doing a film score if I could get one. I'd like to do a film score. Somebody offered me a theme for a television show which I'm not very sure I want to do. I would like to do a real nice film score though. I'd like to get my teeth into something like that. The performing is really fun and I enjoy doing it. I'm glad everybody likes it, I like it too, but as far as I'm concerned, that's not really where it's at.

"My first love," Barry clearly stated, "is being a musician and that's where I'm most comfortable. Getting out there in my glitter clothes, and talking and carrying on; it's part of what I do, but it's not really the most of it. The most fun I have is when I'm in the studio, and when I'm working with a whole bunch of musicians."

"How did you get started in commercials?" I asked next.

"When I was coaching the singers, I had written a song which one of the singers that I was coaching decided to put on a reel of tape. He was going to show it around to various commercial agencies so he could get a job as a commercial singer. I think they hired him for that, and at the same time they asked who wrote that particular song. He gave the agency my number, and they called me. And . . . I started working for them as a writer, and finally a singer.

"Basically I had a pretty hot streak, on commercials as a writer and as a singer. By that time I decided that I enjoyed singing and I also decided that you made more money from singing commercials than you do from writing them. So, it was a combination of writing, arranging, and singing jingles from one of the other, or all three. They would hire me to do either one.

"I sang a lot of them and I wrote a few, I wrote the 'State Farm Insurance' thing, and the 'Stridex' thing, 'Band-Aids,' a couple of car commercials, 'McDonald's' and the 'Pepsi.' The way that I got that . . . they call you, for instance: they asked me to write that 'Pepsi' thing and they had gotten it down to like three different versions and mine was one of them. They finally selected Ellen Starr's version of it. It's the same lyric, only everybody puts a different melody."

"That was 'The Pepsi Generation?'" I inquired.

"Yeah, this was the 'Feeling Free' thing," Manilow continued. "So, when they got it down to those three, I was singing everybody's versions! We all had sung on each other's versions. So, whoever they picked, we would all sing on it! So, that's how I got that job, and most of them are like that. Same thing with the 'Dr. Pepper' thing, I had written my version of 'Dr. Pepper,' and again it got down to like five different versions, and Randy Newman's was one of them. And, they picked the Randy Newman version, but since I had sung on Randy Newman demos, I got to sing on the final ones too! That's how most of them were. They were all different agencies. In the beginning, there was one, but near the end of them . . . you see I don't do commercials anymore; I just have no time . . . but, before I started going on the road it was about five different agencies."

Interested in finding out more about the song that "broke" him to the national audience in a huge way, I questioned, "When 'Mandy' came out, was there a big promotion push?"

"There was of course the usual promotion push," he told me. "Arista has to make it known that there is a product to be played. The minute people played it, it went faster than anything! I haven't been involved with anything other than Bette's career. I have never seen a record go like that, in my life! That record was jumping twenty, thirty points a week, and it went 'Number One' in five,six weeks. All of a sudden it was just all over. I just could not turn the radio on without hearing it, and we'd just released it!"

"Was your head spinning?" I asked.

"Oh, no! It was spinning afterwards," he anwered. "It wasn't spinning then . . . it was like it wasn't happening to me! I was getting these numbers over the phone, and I was saying, 'How nice.' Nobody knew who 'I' was!"

I interjected, "You mean, 'Whoever it is . . . *I like it!*'"

"Yeah!" Barry laughed, *"Nobody* knew who 'I' was! I was going to be an arranger if Bette's thing didn't work out. I was going to go to Liza Minnelli or something. I was going to be an arranger and conductor . . . different course. Who'd have thunk? I tell you, fate works in strange ways don't it?" he snickered.

The next evening was to be the closing night of the 1975 summer season of outdoor concerts in Wollman Skating Rink, and part of a series sponsored by The Schaffer Beer Company. To close the season, Melissa Manchester shared the bill with Barry for a Friday night performance.

"The Schaffer thing tomorrow," Manilow previewed of his ensemble, "we've only got an hour, because Melissa's opening. So we're not going to do the two-acter; the two act concert. We're going to do the one hour thing, so that limits us. I want to do the stuff that the people have come to hear, and I also want to show them some of the new things. Sort of an abbreviated version of what I would do if I had a full evening. Melissa and I are going to do a duet; and do *two* duets! We rehearsed on it all week and stuff. It's nice! You coming to it?"

There wasn't a chance of my having missed it. Not only did I witness the result of Manilow's sudden metamorphosis into a brightly-winged headlining entertainer, but I also experienced around me that night the undying devotion of Manilow fans, strongly evident even at that early stage of his solo career . . . only eight months after "Mandy" was the nation's "Number One" song.

That cold and raining September Friday night in Central Park, a shivering mob huddled against each other for warmth, and waited for a matter of hours to see Barry Manilow. It is indeed extraordinary to see people patiently freezing under umbrellas, some with their feet in inches of water, or seated on soggy newspapers, waiting for the show to start . . . late, and still have everything but their spirits dampened.

Testing out the then-unreleased "Bandstand Boogie" in front of the moist masses, he had thousands rocking in the rain. Barry introduced the song with the factually-based statement, "You have to have been raised in Yugoslavia to have not heard of American Bandstand!" After Manilow's solo set, Melissa Manchester came out on stage again to join him for a duet final medley of Motown classics, "My Girl" and "My Guy." It was a fitting ending.

IV
THUNDERBOLTS:
Lady Flash on Barry Manilow

Sashaying towards an audience in a flurry of fabric, come forth three flowing figures in capes. Stunning an audience both visually and vocally, a crowd rarely knows what has hit them when this tempestuous triad of talent cuts loose. Much to their pleasure, they have been struck by the thunderbolt threesome known as Lady Flash.

Although, three totally separate and uniquely different individuals, they are clearly a unit. Although they were originally "cast" for their roles as a part of Barry Manilow's stage, touring and recording incorporation, it is difficult to believe that they haven't known each other for years!

Once an important part of Barry's whole operation, Lady Flash is now a separate entity unto itself. Just as Bette Midler had suddenly disbanded her troupe after the Palace Theater engagement in 1973, following the last date of his 98-city tour, in April, 1977, Barry and his band, City Rhythm, and his singers, Lady Flash, all amicably parted ways to pursue their own creative capabilities.

Seated across a coffee table cluttered with stacks of music, rock & roll periodicals, and cans of Diet Dr. Pepper, I met Lady Flash an afternoon in June, two months post-Manilow. Their personalities mesh, flow, and overlap. They are politely considerate not to interrupt each other's statements, but they think so much alike that they almost always finish each other's sentences!

They each wore a piece of "Lady Flash Jewelry" on gold chains around their necks—a cloud with a metallic flash of lightning diagonally intersecting it—hanging at the throat.

"Well," Monica began by explaining Lady Flash's emergence, "we're definitely an entity and definitely a group unto ourselves."

"We're writing too!" Reparata announced. "See, the last album, because it was our first album, Barry was the producer, and it was that kind of a vehicle for us, in conjunction with the tour and everything. Barry wrote songs specifically for us and produced it. A lot of people thought that he had the songs in his trunk, but, no, he sat down and he wrote songs for Lady Flash; he had Reparata in mind . . . he had Monica in mind. Of course, you're not going to turn down Barry Manilow material because it's good, but also, we are writing.

"We've absorbed a lot from Barry. We were sort of in 'Star School' with him. We watched him go from an unknown singer; when we were hired he was completely unknown. We got hired to do a four-city tour closing at Carnegie Hall, fall of seventy-four. Then 'Mandy' hit really big, and things just snowballed from there, and we've been working with him ever since. We've backed him up on three albums, and his latest was the live performance at The Uris. But, we've learned a lot, and absorbed a lot, so we're ready to go on our own now. We're definitely ready to do this. Because, you see, the back-up thing for us was a new experience. We were all lead singers before Barry hired us. It wasn't as if we had been going from group to group . . . from Paul Anka . . . to Neil Sedaka, singing back-up. It wasn't that way at all. It was for the first time that we've ever been involved in that area."

Monica cited some examples of former fields of endeavor for the three of them: "Individuals, and jingles and that sort of thing, but never really going out and backing up somebody."

"Luckily for us, it was probably . . . the best . . ." Reparata reconsidered the magnitude of her statement, ". . . it was *the best* back-up job in existence, when we were with Barry, because Barry featured us so heavily. We were really important to the show; important to him."

According to Debra: "He got into a sense of us, as opposed to just hiring three women and having them stand in the background and singing 'oooooo's' and 'aaahhhhh's.' He got into Monica, and Reparata, and Debra as friends, as co-workers, and he realized that he had some talent on his hands, so he felt that he wanted to feature us. It was time for him in his mind . . . which makes him very secure to do that . . . because we've heard background singers say that they sing behind the curtain! They'd say, 'You are sooo lucky, we can't even dance because we dance better than the star, so they made us stop dancing . . . made us *stop* doing things!' We realized that it was very lucky that we got that kind of thing."

"Right," agreed Reparata. "Sharing the spotlight is something that Barry knows how to do, and still maintain himself as a focus because he's secure in what he does, and we're secure in what we do. So there's not that kind of a competition, that you would feel. He was the one that really prompted us, prodded us into recording. He's the one that said, 'Let's take the girls into the studio and do an album.' "

"It didn't take too much prodding I must say!" Monica exclaimed.

Deborah demonstrated, "Do I stand here? That's all you needed to know!"

"That's really when Lady Flash became a group," Monica pointed out. "We didn't intend for it to be this way. We all started out not knowing each other when we auditioned for him, and all that sort of thing. But, it was then that the group started evolving. I guess it was a matter of seeing the opportunities too. Of couse, you can't not see that, but settling with the fact that we could do it with each other. See, there could be loads of opportunities, but if you feel awful with who you're working with, then you don't care. You don't really care, you know that you'll get it some kind of way anyway, so that was really when it started for us as a separate entity."

Reparata strongly feels that the present is proper for Lady Flash establishing themselves: "We feel that the time is definitely right for us. There's a void in the music industry as far as female groups; contemporary women ... women representing women in music. It is just not around. There just isn't anybody doing that, so that will be an important thing for us to do. There's already a space there. It's there, we're just stepping into our allotted space."

Says Monica of the direction that they will take, "We have been told lately, 'Well, you ladies are going to have to make an artistic decision as to how you want to break. Because of the content of the group, because there are two black ladies, and one white lady in the middle ... and the kind of music, and who you want to get across to.' I just think that we can't help believe that there is a way to combine the resources, and put it into an area that everybody will be able to feed off of. That's tough, and we admit that, but it can happen!"

"There's a way to be versatile," Reparata pointed out. "A lot of acts fail at versatility because they are only what they are. We are three of what we are ... so our scope is wide, by the fact that we're three different people; and three sounds and three voices ... and *one* when we want to be one! Our options are so much greater musically, and our backgrounds are different. Debra studied opera, and she's into classical. Monica's jazz and blues ... and I'm the sixties, and other things. Also, we've all had classical training. We're well-rounded musically, and we would hate to be stuck in a groove ... no pun intended ... on record!" she laughed. "You know ... stuck in a slot. People always want to do that because it's familiar and it's a good reference point for them. But, maybe we could be the new reference point for everybody else."

Explaining their break with Barry, Debra announced, "Our Declaration of Independence Day was ... " (mimicking a bugler's fanfare) "...Taataatataaa!... April thirteenth, nineteen-seventy-seven. It was our last date with Barry in Las Vegas, and it all fell into line; right into place. Barry at that time said, 'Well everybody, I don't know when I'm going back on the road. So, so-long! to the band, the crew, the whole works.' The band had been with him for three years, so we had been through all of this. We have been working our way into becoming our own separate entity all along, so for Lady Flash this wasn't: 'O.K. . . . let's be a group on April thirteenth! O.K.?!' It wasn't like that," she laughs. "It wasn't like that! The timing was so right . . . it was just time for us."

Reparata burst into the conversation bubbling with Andy Hardy optimism, "I've got an *idea*!!! Let's be a group . . . *in this barn*!!!" (Everybody cracked up.)

"We've decided to take advantage of that," Debra continued. "We knew that all of it was falling together for a purpose, and it was time for us to be. So, it felt great, and the parting of the ways was friendly, *very* friendly. Barry said, 'Go with my blessings!' So, that's what happened."

"You know," Reparata interjected, "it's interesting to note that there's a parallel here between us, and Barry and Bette that's been pointed out. Bette Midler took a vacation, and that was when Barry said, 'Well, I think I'll put my act together.' . . .and the rest is history! It's sort of the same thing. Barry said, 'I'm going to take off.' It's not a question of anybody getting fired, or we saying, 'We're leaving you!' It was just, 'Well, I guess we have some months . . . .' It was a natural evolution. Also, Barry saw Bette rise to stardom. He was right there with her at The Continental Baths. And, we saw *him* skyrocket too!"

Beginning with Debra, the three members of Lady Flash gave me their three totally different life stories. Debra unraveled her personal yarn.

"Let's see, I started my voice lessons at age twelve, and my piano lessons at age six, even though I can't play too well. I'm not a virtuoso you see, I never will be—but, I've got enough under my belt. I grew up wanting to be an opera star." She reconsiders her aspiration, " . . . *The* new black opera star, of course! But, Grace Bumbry beat me to it! I broadened my musical scope, and I wanted to delve into other parts of music: gospel and rock, and theater. In my growing-up ages I was involved in courses and all that kind of thing, and all of the while having music theory and music shoved down my throat. But, I loved it, I really wanted to do that, and I took to that easily. I guess I just thought I was born to do music. In Cleveland, I went through the high school stages in various groups; local groups and things that I had thrown together, and whatnot. And, I went to Kent State University as a 'music theory major.' I came out of there and I got involved in theater. I decided, 'Well, I'll try theater, and my acting abilities.' I got involved in directional trainings and on-stage dealings, and I enjoyed that very much.

"I incorporated my music into that acting experience, and I became a musical director, for musicals. And after doing everything I could possibly do in Cleveland; the jingles ... how many jingles, and commercials, and television, and radio, and throwing shows together can you do? So, I auditioned here in New York for the Broadway musical "Raisin." I got the audition in Cleveland. This was through my theater workings. People who had passed through my shows. I was given the principal role Ruth Younger, and I moved to New York. I drove a truck there!

"I got here," Debra continued, "and the young lady I was to replace, decided that she didn't want to leave yet! She was going to the hospital and she was going to leave the show for good, and she said, 'Oh, I won't go yet.' And I said, 'What do you mean you won't go yet!?! I just moved all of my things out here.' Like Reparata said, 'I almost *put* her in the hospital!'

"While waiting for her to leave, I started auditioning around New York . . . that was my taste of beating the pavement. I wore out a couple pair of shoes doing that. And through all of this, I had auditioned for Barry Manilow. I answered an ad in the 'trades,' in *Backstage* that said, 'MANILOW NEEDS GIRLS,' and the job description: 'Must move well. Must sing rock & roll.' I said, 'People *sing* rock & roll? What is that?' I couldn't remember what 'rock & roll' was! So, I said, 'I'm singing this.' I didn't know if it was rock & roll . . . and it wasn't! Nobody else at the audition sang rock & roll either. When I walked in the audition, there was this room full of girls, over in the corner going, 'Aaaaaaaaaaaaaaaaah!' and 'Mimimimimimimimimi!' '' (Debra demonstrates vocal exercises.) "That's always hysterical to look at, because I have this confidence thing when I go into auditions. I walked in, I signed my paper. I was 'Number 165,' and I asked the young lady there, 'Who is Barry Manilow?' She said, 'You don't know who Barry Manilow is?!' I said, 'No, I'm sorry . . . ' She never explained to me either, as a matter of fact, who he was!

"So, I went in and I sang for him, and he was sitting at a table with four or five people, two ladies I remember, and a couple of guys. I looked at all of these young people, and I said, 'I don't know who he is still.' He couldn't be the ladies . . . so, I sang my audition thing, and he stopped me in the middle of it and he said, 'Wait a minute! I want you to go out, and I'm going to put you with two other girls.' So that's what let me know, and I said,

'You're Barry?' And he said, 'O,K.!' So, I went out of the room, and he put me with two other young ladies and I came back in, because he wanted to hear blendings and whatnot, and I got to the piano, and he got his music there. Somebody else was playing the piano, and he did a couple. 'It's a Miracle' I sang, I remember, and 'Sweet Life.' I was singing with these other two ladies, and I can't remember who they were. I saw the music with his name on it. I said, 'You write this stuff?' He said, 'Yeah.' I said, 'This is *good stuff* here!' He said, 'Thank you.' and I said 'This is *really* good!' I remember saying that to him, and I walked back.

"I found out later from Reparata ... " she revealed, " ... I came back for the 'Call Backs,' and that's where I saw Reparata for the very first time, and I didn't know he wanted a particular color combination. But, Reparata was the only white girl there, so I figured, 'Well, she must have the job!' And, it seems that he had chosen me. Reparata, me, and another young lady were at the call backs, and then we started putting our 'looks' together. I came in with my best secretary suit from Cleveland, Ohio, and that's gray. And, my flip ... *very* 'mid-western,' you know! Barry started working on the 'look' of us. Rep would get into her 'look.' Barry had a sense of ... he wanted glamour in his show. I said, 'Well, I can start with eyelashes, I've been wearing eyelashes since I was seventeen.' That was no problem.

"But, when we would get ready to do shows, he would say, 'Debra, your make-up is too tasteful. You have the look of a secretary.' I said, 'Well, O.K., what changes do you want?' 'MORE RED! Red here!' " (stroking her cheek) " 'Red here!' " (outlining her lips).

"We were in the dressing room having this tug-o-war: 'MORE RED!' 'NO!!!' 'YES!!! You need MORE RED!' And this was upsetting to me. This was on the road, at our third gig. But we went through our first weeks, and whatnot."

However Reparata points out of their appearance, "Everybody was too busy to notice! And, we were singing very gently."

Debra reinforces, "We were singing gently . . . yes; because we were singing this close . . . " (Instantaneously, on cue, they huddled shoulder-to-cheekbone on the couch before me, to illustrate the cramped quarters of the first tiny club stages) " . . . doing choreography, you see. I would hit Reparata, she would hit me back. I would hit the bass player in the head. Barry had to duck, because I was this close to him . . . " (Debra swings her arm out in demonstration) "That was the club set up. You try to get three ladies, one man with a piano, four guys in the band, on a stage about as big as this table . . . " (Motioning to the cluttered two-foot by three-foot coffee table in front of her) " . . . you have a really hard job."

"Barry did it!" Rep credited.

"And we were dancing and ducking speakers like this . . . and just the coming into each other was an experience! I respected Barry as a musician more than anything else, and I said that to him at rehearsal before we went on the road. He had a great sense of himself. What he wanted his show to be. You know how you wait to feel people out . . . that was my first reaction to him: my musician respect. I guess because I was so into the whole 'musical director' aspect, and after finding out more background about Barry, I realized where my respect came from. His dealings, his arranging, his past, and mine were similar. So, that was common ground. He and I had musician respect. Even without getting to know the person. Then to get into the person, and you become buddies, and the whole deal. And those are my Barry Manilow beginnings," she concluded.

Next to tell her tale was Monica: "I guess the most important thing in my career was the club thing," she began, "because that is where I developed whatever persona I have on stage, of which, it has to be 'me.' Like Debra, I came from the theater. She did loads and loads of theater. I did some of it, and I didn't stay, just simply because I didn't have that 'passion.' But, I loved being able to try my personality out on people. You don't get a chance to do that as freely in any other place as you do in a club. And, I really got off on doing that. I got off on pulling on other people's personalities as well. I studied. I studied privately; I didn't go to college. I sang with a group called The Voices Of East Harlem for two years. That was a different experience. That was singing with ten thousand people! . . . as opposed to singing by yourself, which is a total turn-around; but it was a rich experience. I did two albums with them. We toured Europe. Seeing the contracts was more of an experience than the actual doing it. And, The Black Experience, of course. Being involved in that sort of thing. Dabbling in and out of different areas as far as what kind of music is concerned. I love singing show tunes. I loved taking a song, and making it another kind of music. I liked jazz. I liked Motown. I was a Motown kid! I mean, I was *a Motown kid*!!! It was for a good reason, because they have turned out things: premises and ideas in music. I'm really happy that I experienced that era.

"My parents were in show business. That was a very, very rich experience for me. I just remember being on the road with them and going through it. You know, a child picks up and feels what you're feeling without knowing why. So, there are many experiences that are a part of me, that I didn't actually experience in a physical sense. I remember my mother and father being picked up at train stations, by local sheriffs of some local torn-down Southern town, because they were black. And being taken to a designated spot, and being told to sing, and being taken back to the train station, and being told to 'Get out of town!' And, I remember all of that stuff. So, that stuff was really rich and . . ." she stresses; of performing, " . . . that's really doing it because you *like* to do it! That's really doing it because you just have that passion for it! So, that kind of stuff. I think the biggest influence in what I bring to Lady Flash, is my mom. I don't know how or why, but I think it's just that 'aura,' that I picked up from her: the taste in music, the way I would like to convey it with Lady Flash. It's part of me, and I think it has a lot to do with that."

Monica analyzed further, "It's definitely from within, that I'm now beginning to realize that I picked up all of that stuff then. Of course it was always there. You're a product of everything that you've experienced, or everything that you've ever thought. Now, I'm starting to use those things, and it's really nice.

"The nightclub thing; again, I got back into after I left The Voices Of East Harlem, and I did that here." She reflects of the New York nightspots she had worked at, "You know; Reno Sweeney's, and Grand Finale, and that circuit. Which is hard to pay the rent all the time . . . in that circuit. And, that's where I auditioned for Barry Manilow. Barry's manager, Miles Lourie, heard me singing there, at Reno Sweeney's. I was looking for management at the time, and he and I, because of that . . . had a history. About a year later, after he had heard me, the idea of auditioning for Barry came to my attention. And, of course, I had my nose up in the air: 'Singing back-up!?!' But, I must have been doing it for a reason. Just going where the flow was!"

On her actual Manilow audition, Monica remembers, "I auditioned for him, and I was the last person to audition; I replaced another lady. I came in at the end of the audition day. I walked in, and there they were, in this little corner here, The Flashy Ladies . . . as they were then called, getting ready to do Musical Chairs. There were other people who were in the back who were auditioning and trying on clothes after they got done singing. There was all of this activity going on when I came in. But, the immediate feeling (from Barry) was: 'warmth.' That was the *immediate* feeling . . . I got 'person' . . . I got 'Well, I know what I'm doing and I know what my expertise is and all of that; but I'm bringing the human element into it as well.' Not everybody does that, and that was the first thing that I was impressed with about Barry. And the music too, I remember Rep said to me, 'You're going to like the music!'

"He started doing some things, and I was just totally impressed with him. The persona of bringing everybody into your space, and having them enjoy it too. Allowing everybody living within the confines of them having to do what you want them to do, but being themselves. He was good at that. It's not easy, I wouldn't think, to allow everybody to be their own person, and still working for someone else. He always allowed for that. There were times when he didn't and shouldn't have; as a leader, but he seemingly believed in that from the very beginning, and that's what happened."

During the spring of 1976, Monica and Barry shared a very adventurous, personally self-improving venture. Together, they sought help for their habitual cigarette smoking. As Monica tells the episode, "Barry and I went to Smoke Enders together. Barry used to smoke Pall Mall without a filter. If you never smoked cigarettes, it seems futile to even discuss it. We learned at Smoke Enders that people are divided into only a few groups. 'One' is the people who never smoke at all, never smoked before, and they can't figure out why people start in the first place. 'Two' is the people who are still smoking, who say, 'Oh, she's so self-righteous!' And, 'Three' is people who have quit 'cold turkey,' and say, 'Haa, you need something else to help you quit . . . you're *weak*!'

"Barry and I were people who, no matter what we had to do, would just pick up a cigarette. Barry smoked Pall Mall cigarettes; I smoked two-and-a-half packs a day! We were both just walking chimneys when we went there! We were like two scared kids, and the most I can say for it was that it gave me insight into Barry, the person, and him into me . . . because, things had to be bared there. I imagine it's something like EST, you really have to bare yourself . . . to yourself there.

"After the first week, he called me, and he said, 'Monica, do you feel dumb?' and I said, 'Yes, I feel like a complete fool for smoking cigarettes.' "

Monica explained about their experience to-gether: "We both really gained some insight into

having something lead you around; and letting
something master you, rather than you mastering
it. It was really interesting, and our biggest fear was
. . . because this was basically during the time that
Lady Flash was recording an album . . . which was
a fine time to stop smoking as far as your nerves
are concerned! But, before we went out on the road
for the next tour and our biggest fear was, 'My
God Barry: can you see us not smoking a cigarette
before going on stage?! Can you see yourself *not*
lighting up that cigarette, just to cool yourself out?'
And, I said, 'Evidently we're going to be doing it
. . . huh?' " She laughs, ". . . and *we did!*"

After Monica was finished telling her story
about Smoke Enders, she and Debra left their pub-
licist's offices to run afternoon errands. Their exit
afforded Reparata full use of the stage to elaborate
on "The Lady Flash Legend," and recreate the
dramatic conversion of "Lorraine Mazolla of
Brooklyn to Reparata of The Delrons."

"I'm from Brooklyn, New York," she began.
"In my family were musicians, but, not professionally. It was in those days that you *never* were
a musician for a living, because you couldn't make
that much. And, anyway, 'respectable people'
didn't play music! My father became a banker, and
he played excellent guitar. And my uncle became
something else, and he played sax. I always was
surrounded by live music, and I was the only sev-
en-year-old torch singer . . . in the world! I was
singing all of these hot lyrics, 'Some Of These
Days' and 'Ballin' The Jack,' and everything . . .
and I was seven-years-old! All I knew was the
lyrics, I didn't know what they meant! My
background is very musical in that respect.

"When my father died, my mother, who was also

a trained concert pianist before she married, taught music after he died. So, I was surrounded by all sorts of things going on. And, when I was in high school, I was in all of the glee clubs, and choirs, and things like that. In my freshman year, for The Freshman/Senior Talent Party, I sang "Some Of These Days" *a cappella,* in an all-girls school . . . run by nuns. So it didn't make such a good impression for the next four years . . . I didn't know what I was doing! I knew I wanted to sing, and that was the only important thing to me.

"At the beginning of my college years, I joined the group Reparata and the Delrons. When I came into the group I was not the lead singer, but the girl who was the lead singer got married, and left the business. She's a teacher. Before I joined it was Reparata and the Delrons, so that's how I took the name. We looked around for a lead singer, but nobody seemed to find anybody, so I took over the lead, and that's how that whole thing evolved. That was in 1969; I became Reparata in 1969. We had done a tour of England, and the group was successful, but I was raised in the school of, "if you want a career, you *don't* do it singing!' It's 'something else.' So, I graduated from Brooklyn College. I have a degree in French, and a Masters in television, and I decided, at least if I can't be in front of the camera, at least be connected with the business, behind the scenes. Until . . . I realized after a while, that was an avocation; television. My real love was singing!

"I was working and singing and writing, and doing all of these things, and my mother was going bananas; saying, 'Why are you doing this?' . . . 'Why are you spreading yourself so thin? . . . Give up the business! . . . What are you crazy?' And, I kept saying, '*No,* I must go on!' So, in great dramatic tradition, when I was in college . . . I was singing rock & roll *undercover*. I was in The Baroque Choir, and the choirmaster didn't approve of anything but Baroque music, so I used to sneak off and sing rock 'n' roll with The Delrons.

"Reparata and her Delrons, Mary Aiese, and Nanette Licari, ended up surprising everyone in the end, as they harmonized their way into a recording deal. They were a brief smash on this side of the Atlantic with a pair of pop hits, 'Tommy' and 'When A Teenager Cries.' However, it was England that they broke the biggest . . . especially in May, 1967, when the group's single 'Captain Of My Ship' was the 'Number One' there!

"I had been on tour with Reparata and the Delrons in England, which was kind of unrealistic because we were three young girls, protected and locked in our hotel room. We never saw our money. The typical sixties syndrome: the managers . . . and what they did to you in the sixties. The stories are all true, from my experience. Maybe there were some great managers in the sixties, but *we* didn't have one, and we got taken advantage of. Probably because we were women, and that's changed definitely. We're learning how to be the boss now, which is hard for women anyway . . . but in those days there was no question!"

Reparata discussed the financial aspect of the Delrons' tour: "We got a lot of money . . . we never saw any of it, and we left our first tour *in debt!* We really didn't want to go, we said, 'I don't want a release. I don't really want to see England!' I was engaged, I didn't want to leave my house! They said, 'Well, go on this tour, at least you won't have to spend money . . . it'll be a promotional tour.'

Well . . . we came back *owing nine hundred dollars*. They had to book us back just because we had to pay off our debts!"

Just to set the facts straight, I asked Reparata if she eventually married the gentleman to whom she was engaged in 1967?

"Oh, no!" she exclaimed, "*nothing* ever worked out right in the sixties!

"When the group broke up, I was still working in television, and I decided to put a tape together for myself, to try and get jingle work, and things around the city. And, Barry's girlfriend, Linda Allen was the executive producer at CBS where I worked. I was a producer . . . I made it in television, I made it pretty well. And, everybody thought I was nuts for giving up my career in television. I got an Emmy nomination for 'Best Informational Talk Show Series,' which was a local talk show on the air here (in New York City), 'The Pat Collins Show.' We lost, but it didn't matter to me . . . by that point I'd already left television. The Emmy nomination came out when I was on the road. It was really funny!

"I met Barry through Linda Allen. She knew that I was Reparata, and Bette was looking for Harlettes at the time, so she gave my tape to Barry, and I auditioned for Bette. But, I did not happen to get the job, for whatever reason it was. I don't know, I never really talked to him about it in detail. I didn't get the job. I guess it wasn't time . . . whatever it was. But, a year later, when he was putting his own girls together, he decided to call me for an audition. He remembered my tape, so I auditioned for him. I remember the audition. The audition was held in his apartment. I never really knew Barry that well, I produced the show with him, when he was just starting. I saw Barry's first live performance ever, at The Continental Baths. It was a showcase for him, for the record companies. I remember him coming out with his blonde hair and all in white. Really, it was something to see even in those days!

"The show was called 'Barry Manilow And Friends,' " Rep elaborated, " . . . that was how it was billed, and he had all of his friends singing! I got the job, and that's where I met Debra. I loved Barry Manilow's music . . . I mean I just thought to myself, 'This must be heaven, because if I have to be singing rock, I don't want to be singing music that's the 'screamer' type of thing!' I like Barry's music . . . I really do, and I like him, and the thing that Debra was talking about . . . when Debra and I first met each other, it was like we had known each other our entire lives. And that's the way the whole Barry Manilow tour went. You see, Barry is very special in that he wants talented people around him that will get along. He doesn't need that dissension. You see, 'the tone is set at the top,' because he is the way he is. He wants people around him to be nice people, because no working situation is really productive if you're going to have all those stupid, petty tensions on the road. And, eventually Barry developed a little family around him. I mean, we would kill for Barry Manilow . . . if, God forbid, anybody should come near him, or say anything about him! It's a very tight-knit family, which showed on stage. The rapport between Barry and us, and Barry and the band, and the whole thing was 'a family.' I mean, if we can live together three years on the road, and make it through alive . . . and *still* be friends!

"As I said, I left this very promising career in

television, and everybody thought I was a lunatic, because I was going with an unknown artist on a four-week tour which closed at Carnegie Hall. Barry said, 'Look, I can't promise you any more than what's booked.' Philadelphia, Boston, Nashville, Memphis; we were playing *all* clubs . . . The Bijou, Paul's Mall, The Exit Inn, and Lafayette Music Hall. A couple of them aren't even there anymore . . . *and* closing at Carnegie Hall in November. So, I said, 'I've never seen those cities; that would be nice. And singing in Carnegie Hall certainly sounds very interesting to me!'

"So, I left television," Reparata continued. "I figured I could tell everybody I went on vacation, and get another job. As it turned out, as we were on the road, 'Mandy' was snowballing. We did the things . . . like in Boston, we sat on the phone calling, 'Oh, would you play that record by Barney Mantelobe? ' . . . you know, phoning radio stations and things that you do in the beginning, when you struggle. And, the thing snowballed to a phenomenon! Barry's had, I don't know how many records; 'Gold' albums, 'Platinum' albums . . . but, it's well-deserved, because the thing that impresses me about Barry is: Number One . . . Barry knows how to anticipate trends. We saw it when he would say to us, 'Those shoes, with the spike heels that you don't want to wear, everybody's going to be wearing them soon.' Sure enough. The next thing we know, 'You have to put your eyes like this, because that's going to be very big. Women are going to be doing that.'

"He did that with music, he did that with his whole, entire act, he did that with his style of music. He's always anticipated trends. He's always one step ahead. Innovative. He's also the first person I've seen, as far as live production, who can *see* a song on stage, as well as how it's going to sound! Most musicians are just concerned with what it's going to sound like. Barry is also concerned with the 'look' of a song . . . the choreography . . . the staging, and that is from theater background. Barry was in the theaters of New York for a long time before he ever thought of becoming a solo artist.

"Another thing about working with Barry as a producer in the studio, was that Barry cared about 'seeing' the artist on a record. More like being a director in the theater, rather than just sitting in a booth, just listening to sounds . . . technically. He would say, 'I'm closing my eyes, and I don't see Reparata singing. I don't feel that you believe that line . . . ' And, you know; if you've spent a lot of time listening to Barry Manilow's records, his phrasing; he's really a good storyteller, and that's what I learned from him in the studio. He's also a perfectionist, which people often times confuse with temperament. Being professional has gotten a bad name. You're 'hard to work with' because you want the right thing. I'm sure Streisand has the same problem. But, I've learned a lot from him. I've absorbed a lot. Assimilated it, and it will definitely manifest itself in the Lady Flash act, because there are certain things that you don't do when you're on stage.

"Barry of course, comes from Brooklyn," Reparata mentioned proudly, "and Barry and I have a special thing there, because we share a very common background, and we're very good friends to this day. I'm still protective of him. I don't care if he is a star. He's my friend now, and I'll have to take care of him. He's very important to me still.

It's the level of professionalism that Barry has. His level is really high for everyone on that show. His audition, he wants everybody to work only as hard as he does. Which is like . . . 'You'd have to be a madman to work *only* as hard as he does!' If you can do the job, then you can get his respect. 'Respect' I think is the key word all around. He respects talent. He respects people, and he answers his fan mail personally if he feels that they need the help. If you want to put it simply, Barry Manilow is human. He's sincere, and it sounds . . . sacchariny . . . to say that, and I'm sure that everybody is going to say the same thing. You're not going to find too much bad-mouthing about Barry Manilow. There isn't anything to say except good things. He's a real artist. What can I say? . . . I'm his 'Number One Fan!'

"We're still good friends, and what he gave Lady Flash to take with them. We used to do interviews with him, he'd say, 'Remember, you're taking a piece of me with you!' and we'd say, 'Well, Barry . . . what piece are we taking? Give us a *good* piece, please!' He was interested, and the break as we said, was amicable. It's just a matter that we both feel it's just the best thing to do now . . . for both of us. He doesn't have the time, and we would really like to be ourselves."

Rep informed me that, "Lady Flash will really branch out into different areas, because of our backgrounds. We're going to do it! I mean with Debra's theater training, and my television, I mean . . . I know how to write camera directions! I've already got the sheet with camera directions. I want them to know when they have to shoot wide. Because people miss the choreography, that's annoying to me."

Now you've got to admit . . . that's one 'ready-for-anything' lady . . . . she even carries her own television camera directions!

"Monica helps with the clubs," she continued, "and it's really fortunate that it's the three of us together. A lot of people have said it before, but we really do get along. We meditate together before we go on. We are a definite unit . . . we're individuals . . . three separate personalities. Before Monica came into the group, there wasn't that group feeling."

There was an evolution in the ultimate structure of Lady Flash that occurred in between the "Tryin' To Get The Feeling" album, and the "This One's For You" album. On the former, Barry's back-up trio was sub-titled "The Flashy Ladies," on the latter they were already, officially "Lady Flash." The difference in the two incarnations found the addition of Monica Burress to the group's line-up, as she replaced the original third girl.

Reparata filled in the blanks: "A girl by the name of Ramona Brooks. She's singing out-of-town. The circumstances of her leaving were sad; she had a throat problem. She felt she really should leave and rest her voice. So it wasn't really that she was fired or anything like that . . . but when Monica came in . . . 'it' was there!

"On August 15, 1975, Monica came in for her audition. That's the birth of Lady Flash as we know it. I'm glad. We've all been in groups, and I guess we were a little bit leery at first, since we were singing solo things . . . Monica was singing solo. And, I agree that if it hadn't been with these two ladies, I don't know whether I'd want to be in a group again. It's a lot of problems. It's a group, but each member of the group is allowed to develop first of all. Usually in a group, you're stifled—there's usually a lead who overshadows the other two. In this case: All leads . . . raise your hand . . . and all of us raise our hands! If I didn't feel like I was in a situation where I could grow, I don't think I would be here. I think I would be doing something else. But fortunately, there's no competition intramurally; we're different. I don't have to try and sing better than Debra, she sings differently. People make that mistake anyway in all phases of life, not just this particular group. They're always looking at somebody else, instead of seeing if they can be best. It's another sense of knowing yourself, trying to look inside instead of pulling from the outside. Pulling up and outward, and we all know that too. I think that the time is right. The industry's there. The timing, the void in the business, Barry's contribution, what we will develop into—It's *perfect*!

"We're all supposed to be in this place. It's no accident that it all started. I don't feel that it will be an accident; and I don't feel that it's going to be unsuccessful either, because all of the circumstances are right."

Back to Barry, Rep resumed, "As you can see, we loved working with him, and we knew it was special when it was happening, which is fortunate because Barry and I used to look at each other and say, 'this is unbelievable!' We enjoyed it when it was happening, because we knew that no matter how good it is, that we never would have a job quite like that again . . . with the combination of people. And, the excitement of people discovering Barry Manilow, and then going from the stages of nothing . . . to people discovering."

In the beginning of Barry's touring, there were

sometimes "half houses," or even less. As Reparata disclosed, "We had this rule, we wouldn't go out if the band outnumbered the audience. It's true, we used to play places where I would sit out front on a stool and count, 'One, two, three . . .' In the beginning in clubs, nobody knew who he was in Denver! It was incredible! Now . . . everybody's heard of him, but in the beginning, it was: 'Barry who?' "

Reparata recalls that, "Bill Crystal tells a story about when we did some dates with him in the midwest, and I think 'I Write The Songs' was 'Number One' at the time. And, we pull up to the date . . . and on the marquee, his name is spelled 'BERRY MANTELOBE!' So, Barry said, 'Well, that just brings you back to reality!'

"The road was fun too . . . hard; but . . . a lot of baloney sandwiches in the beginning. We saw ourselves go from baloney sandwiches to Kentucky Fried Chicken, to full course dinners with Shrimp Newberg. As Barry got bigger and bigger, the combinations got better. Well, I'm glad, because Lady Flash is sort of back at the Kentucky Fried Chicken stage. That's O.K., we're prepared. A lot of people who come off of a huge tour like we came off of would be spoiled. We had the reality of knowing where we are that way, and seeing Barry back then. So, we know what to expect—it's so much easier when you know!

"Barry's got a real sense of how things should be done, and as I say, there's that thing: 'temperament' versus 'perfection.' There are temperamental people who ask ridiculous things; you know, 'I want to have my dressing room re-wallpapered before I get in there!' Those stories are true. Barry's stories were, 'I want the sound system to work right! I want the stage to be the right height! I want the dressing room facilities to be good . . . not holes!' "

Just as Barry had emerged onto the popular music scene, charged with crackling sparks of energy from having helped push Bette Midler to the top . . . Lady Flash appears prone to lunge out into the forefront. Their journey on the street to success could realistically take this trio down any or all of the existing entertainment avenue.

Here are Reparata's directions for her closing statement:

—CUT TO: Camera # 2/medium shot of guest
—ZOOM IN/for close-up of guest

REPARATA: "He's just terrific . . . and a talented writer!"

—CUT TO: Camera # 1/close-up shot of interviewer

MARK: "Thank you, Reparata!"

—ZOOM OUT
—CUT TO: Camera # 2/long shot of subjects
—ROLL CREDITS
—FADE TO BLACK
—END.

With three of Bette Midler's original Harlettes, Barry played The Bottom Line, May, 1974, his solo New York City public debut.

Photo by: IDA S. LANGSAM

For career guidance, Barry looks up to his manager Miles Lourie. Here they are seen sharing a laugh at a press conference held before Barry's Christmas 1975 benefit show.

Photo by: IDA S. LANGSAM

Lawrence Welk eat your heart out! Barry bubbles at New York's Beacon Theater, December, 1975.

Photo by: IDA S. LANGSAM

Both native New Yorkers, Barry Manilow and Melissa Manchester started out together on the stairway of success, and neither have stopped climbing for a minute!

Photo by: IDA S. LANGSAM

Prior to the summer of 1976, Barry was always within quick reach of a pack of non-filter Pall Mall's. Having gone without a cigarette at "Smoke Enders," his puffing is a thing of the past.

Photo by: BOBBY BANK

Steppin' out with his ladies! Monica, Barry and Reperata arrive at The Waldorf-Astoria in style. That night he received a "Platinum" album for "Tryin' To Get The Feeling."

Photo by: IDA S. LANGSAM

"Barry's Angels?"...well sort of. *After Dark Magazine* named him "Entertainer Of The Year" in 1976, and shown at the headtable of the reception are: left-to-right (seated) Shirley MacLaine, Barry, and his girlfriend Linda Allen; (standing) Monica Burruss, Reperata, and Debra Byrd.

Photo by: IDA S. LANGSAM

Barry Manilow: "I'm trying to bring back intelligent music; in contrast to noise, in contrast to distortion. Just go get a little more complex, a little more complicated musically and lyrically a little deeper."

Photo by: BOBBY BANK

"New York City Rhythm" at its finest! Barry and his ladies on their own float in The Macy's Thanksgiving Day Parade, November, 1976.

Photo by: TODD WEINSTEIN

With smiles like these, it's no wonder Barry Manilow called them his "flashy ladies." Hence, their name: Lady Flash. Left-to-right they are: Monica Burruss, Reperata, Debra Byrd.

Photo: R.S.O. Records

It was while playing piano for Bette Midler that Barry steered onto the uphill grade to stardom. Bette above, is ready to roll.
Photo by: TOM HILL

This is how Barry appeared on millions of television screens across the world, as he accepted the award for "Record of the Year," for the 1977 Grammy Awards.
Photo by: LARA DONIN

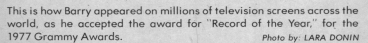

This is a scene from the mammoth stage production that the "Barry Manilow Live" album was taken from. Left-to-right are Monica, Reparata, Debra, Lee Gurst (at the drums), and Barry.

Photo by: LARA DONIN

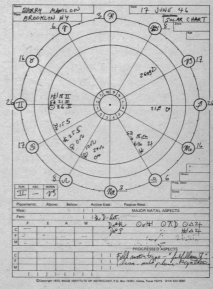

Says astrologer Don Elam of Gemini Barry Manilow's "Solar Chart," "There's an interesting sidelight here. Mars is in 29° Leo. That's in conjuction with fixed star Regulus. This is also what was the ascendant of Franz Liszt, pianist of the last century."

Zodiacal Chart: DON ELAM

V

GROOVING ON BARRY:
By the Man Who First Signed Him to a Recording Contract

"I don't think Barry Manilow is *just* another act. There are a lot of acts that have hit records. They come and they go. I think it would be unfair to name those acts—you know them as well as I do—but this man has been doing it for nigh into three years now, and it's just the beginning! It's getting bigger and bigger and bigger, and it's starting to happen internationally."

The gentleman saying these words from the other side of a large executive desk, speaks freely and with sincerity on the subject of Manilow—and rightfully so. There is no member of the recording industry more directly responsible for Barry's signature first appearing on a solo recording contract, than this man.

The day we met was a clear, semi-torrid Thursday afternoon in August, 1977.

The purpose of my visit was to discuss, from the inner-industry point of view, Barry Manilow's evolution towards his first recording contract as a solo entertainer. Irv Biegel, vice president and partial interest-holder of newly-formed Millinium Records, was my host.

Co-formed by him and his partner Jimmy Ienner, company president, Millinium Records officially began on January 31, 1977. Prior to their partnership, Ienner has best been known for his

production duties with hit-makers like The Rasp-
berries, The Bay City Rollers, and Eric Carmen.
Biegel's last post was with Larry Uttal's company,
Private Stock Records. Prior to July 15, 1974, he
was a top executive at Bell Records, as was Larry
Uttal.

Since establishing Millinium with Jimmy, Irv has
been busily 'anticipating trends,' which seems to
have been his forte for quite some time. He once
sent The Fifth Dimension a song that he knew was
perfect for them. Although they 'yawned' when
they saw it, they recorded it anyway, as a favor to
Irv. The song: "Last Night I Didn't Get to Sleep at
All!" As though their work couldn't be restricted
to the confines of this planet ... it wasn't long
before the label "harnessed the force" with the first
smash—in both album and single form. It was the
instrumental "Star Wars And Other Galactic
Funk" by Meco.

Having seen Barry Manilow on a couple of occasions, it was Irv Biegel who first recognized some
of his yet unexplored capabilities.

Irv Biegel remembered his first encounter with
Manilow:

"Barry Manilow was part of a group that had a
record out on Bell called Featherbed. Don't ask me
the name of the song, because we didn't sell three
copies. Now, later ... the 'B' side of that Featherbed record, was a song called 'Could It Be Magic?'
which was unknown, undiscovered at that time.
We made a one-record deal with Featherbed ... a
single, in fact! I believe Tony Orlando was the
producer of that record. All right, so now Featherbed comes along and nothing happens. Barry comes
back, and he's playing with Bette. He comes
back in with an almost completed master called

'Sweetwater Jones.' He comes in with Ronny Dante, whom I knew much better than I knew Barry. And, they play me three sides that were not totally finished, and I fall in love with it! I really say, hey, this is really sensational. I really want to get involved. So I make one record deal with them, with the option for an album. 'Sweetwater Jones' comes out . . . and nothing happens.

"Barry is now on the road with Bette Midler. I go see Barry—and what he had arranged with Bette is, at intermission, Barry could do two of the three numbers. I see Barry on stage, and I say to myself, 'I think this guy's a *superstar*!' More so, than when I heard the recordings that they came in with.

"In fact, where I first saw them—I went down to Jacksonville, Florida to see them. Now at this time, Barry made one of the best moves he's ever made in his career. He brings in a gentleman named Miles Lourie who was acting as his lawyer, but now becomes his manager . . . O.K.?" Irv punctuated the significance of such a strategy. "And, I think in 'The Barry Manilow Story' . . . the success . . . a lot has to be attributed to Miles Lourie. The way Barry's career was handled: 'with kid gloves!'

"I go down to Jacksonville, Florida and I fall in love with it! And, I come back and they're finishing the tour in New York. It's even better, because the more he's out, the better he is. Then we decide at that point that we're going to go into the Continental Baths where Barry can put on a show, a performance! He's going to put together the girls, he's going to put on. We financed it. I wanted to just bring in some industry people, including a lot of people from my company."

As a by-product of the on-the-road experiences with performing, Irv explains that Manilow had worked to add a fine polish to all of his on-stage elements . . . and it showed!

"We go into the Continental Baths, and when I tell you he kills them—he absolutely fractures them! I mean, unbelievably good! The commercial medley, 'Could It Be Magic', 'I Am Your Child,' these are all things that were on the first album. 'Sweet Life,' which today I swear is a hit record. I love that song! Somebody's going to have a hit with that. We leave the Baths, and I say, 'I'm going to pick up the option now. I want an album!' So, we go in and pick that option which calls for an album."

Biegel points out that the reason for the overwhelming reaction was the fact that his set in Bette's show just allotted him enough time to establish his presence—sing for a few minutes—and leave before reaching any sort of audience rapport. "Remember, when you've seen a guy do three numbers, it's very difficult. Or, two numbers; I think Jacksonville was two. New York was three; because he was known here, for his commercials . . . you know, and he's been around.

"The Baths were just the *most* entertaining, the *most* fun night, the *most* beautiful night of watching an entertainer, as I can remember! We pick up the option. Now, we cut the album, we have to now go to Barry, and we want Barry to go out on tour. O.K.? If we want him to go out on tour, we have to give him money. So, we underwrote the tour, for 'X' amount of dollars. A sizable amount of money at that time. In fact, I will tell you. I don't think it's any big deal. I think it was, fifty-eight or fifty-nine thousand dollars. We knew that the money would be well spent, because Miles is very meticulous and very fastidious when it comes to how the money goes out." Irv pointed out regarding Barry's sensible management.

Between the time of Barry's showcase at the Continental Baths and his embarkment upon his own first tour, was the recording and release of his debut album "Barry Manilow" on Bell Records. Then there were further dates with Bette, including The Palace Theater, Barry and Bette's each going their own separate ways, and his act's dry run at Carroll's Rehearsal Studio. Then it was off on his own!

"The first date was Paul's Mall in Boston, opening for Freddie Hubbard. That's quite a paradox: Barry Manilow and Freddie Hubbard. Now maybe it wasn't the world's best booking," Biegel was the first to admit, "I guess it wasn't; because it's really not the right match. But in the long run, it was the best thing that ever could have happened to Barry, in my mind. Because, the day of the opening, that morning at nine o'clock, Miles calls me, all excited, 'Barry has now panicked! He doesn't want to do it because the sound system is really not up to par, and he's scared. And . . . I understand it. Now you go out there, and you fall flat on your face, or you're going to make it! Knowing now, I realize that it was because Paul's Mall is a jazz club. So Miles says, 'I want you to do me a favor . . .' And, I give a lot of credit to Miles for this. He said, 'Please come up. He likes you, he respects you, and you'll give him confidence.'

"So, we get on an airplane, we go up to Boston, and I do another thing, which I think was fairly bright at the time. I bring up a sound engineer with me, a guy that was working for me and I think he's a very good engineer, by the name of Judd Phillips, who's in the A & R Department (Artists & Repertoire), but his background had been in studio. He's Stu Phillips' nephew and they owned a studio down in Memphis. I bring Judd up; Judd's a very good sound engineer. He goes and looks at the system and makes the corrections, he wants a couple more speakers . . . terrific! Now the sound is good. Barry goes on, and we, being a record company, try to bring in as many people as we can, but we're having great difficulty, so when Barry opens that show, there's like thirty-five people in the audience?"

"And, the capacity of the club?" I asked, wanting a visual conception.

"Two hundred," Irv stated grimly. "That in itself freaked him out. Forty people . . . you know, there are a lot of empty tables. At that point, Barry said, 'This is it, I'm going to do it!' He goes out and he puts on a dynamite show. Absolutely fractures the thirty-five or forty people there . . . O.K.? Now . . . Freddie Hubbard comes on and the club starts to get crowded, because Freddie Hubbard is a very well-known, wonderful jazz artist. But, the next night, those thirty-five people told two hundred people about Barry Manilow. So now, they're not coming in at ten o'clock when Freddie Hubbard comes on . . . they're coming in at eight-thirty or nine o'clock, when Barry comes on. And from there it got better. I don't remember the sequencing of the tour. It went from there to Philadelphia, to Memphis. Every place he went, people just got excited! Absolutely! That commercial medley is a real killer; it's something that people know.

"Barry's got that great wit about him. He's got

that little pixie-ish thing about him. He's a fine, fine musician and a great singer. And the rest . . . obviously is history! I mean; it was a question of progression. The first album was not a great success, but once they re-issued it after his other successes, it's a 'Gold' album. The man is an absolute giant in the industry, and I think this man will be here for twenty years! There's a charm about him, there's a rapport that he creates with an audience. He's very down-to-earth, and relates to the audience, and understands the audience, and knows the difference in audiences—and musically, he's just progressed and progressed."

Already having shown a flair for forecasting the future, Biegel foretold, "I will tell you also one thing that I believe will happen. Barry has not had the monster hits with his own compositions, but that will come. I think Barry is a giant writer. I think he hasn't even scratched the surface yet in that area. I will tell you, 'Could It Be Magic?' for me is one of the classics! No matter how many records it's sold, an incredible adaptation of a classical piece. 'Sweet Life,' 'Mandy' comes along and it's the right song at the right time, and now Barry's off and running. Then it's the Bruce Johnston song. Then he does David Pomeranz's "Tryin' To Get The Feeling,' which is a sensational song, and it's off and running! In between, they release 'It's A Miracle,' which is Barry's song, which does very well. I think they did a half a million singles on that.'

"'Could It Be Magic?' also, the re-cutting of 'Could It Be Magic?' did very well, but then he took off into orbit! And, I'll tell you, I can see this thing lasting . . . not forever, nothing lasts forever. But, as far as being a performer and establishing himself, this man's going to be around for the next twenty-five years! And he'll get better. As good as he is, he's going to get better, because he's matured. He now has much more confidence than he's ever had before, and that has always been a problem with performing artists. It's hard to have confidence in yourself; there's always that insecurity."

Having seen Barry's performing beginnings in-between Bette's stage shows, then to have fronted the money for Barry's own showcase at the Continental Baths, and just to see *if* he could support an entire act as a headliner, Irv is proud to have been instrumental in the outcome. Having seen Barry on Broadway was a great thrill for Biegel to see.

"It's a trip; a real treat to go out and watch this kid perform. Musically, he's sensational and he's vibrant. It's a real sensational evening of music. And I think he reaches a lot of different age groups; he reaches my fourteen-year-old daughter, and there's a ten-year-old kid down the block who wants to go see him, and he also reaches the thirty-five-year-old housewife that goes to see him in Las Vegas. The television shows were really good. *The* television show: it was a *Special*! The next one's going to be sensational. It's just going to be. He's one of those artists. I think he's going to surpass a lot of those other artists that have been fairly prominent in the business today. I think Barry's that much better!

"You see, for me it's really a great thrill, because I was there in the beginning. I happened to be there, and I consider myself fortunate. I also consider myself fortunate because he's a guy that has a long memory of what really happened, and I appreciate the fact that you're here. Obviously, you've heard my name from him and others. I had not been at the record company for three years when that first album was certified 'Gold;' and they sent me a copy of the 'Gold' album! And really, it's the *only* 'Gold' record I've ever kept! I also kept one other thing that has given to me by The Fifth Dimension, and it was called The Golden Ear Award; because I sent them a song called 'Last Night I Didn't Get to Sleep at All,' which," Irv recalls, "they really didn't love! And, they did a very nice thing for me: they presented it to me in Las Vegas when they opened there!"

On the grooming and development of Manilow, Biegel proudly states, "When you see a young man as talented as Barry, your ego gets involved . . . your beliefs. You know, sixty-thousand bucks, or that number approximately, at that time was a lot of money to invest at that time for *our* record company in tour support because of independence. At least our company, was *not* terribly involved in that, and it was a big move for me to make. You know, that's a lot of money. But, you can see it, when you saw it at the Baths. When you saw it, you could see that he turned people on. I mean, forget even having a hit, if we knew we could get that 'word-of-mouth' thing that goes out, it would establish him. And, that's exactly what happened with Barry. I mean he went to Memphis. Nobody knew who he was in Memphis, and all of a sudden, he's booked back. You only get booked back if you're doing business! And it only comes from 'word-of-mouth,' because we were doing very little advertising.

"Most of the tour support came in just giving

him money to pay his band and making sure the bills ... you know, because when you do those kind of tours, you lose money, obviously. You're booked in those clubs for practically 'zip!' And he just grew and grew and grew, and he's going to get bigger! And coming in this morning, 'Looks Like We Made It,' ... you know that's all over the radio! It's a wonderful song! And I really believe songs are so important. I mean, I really believe that's the 'key' to a hit. But it's also 'interpretation,' and he's a great balladeer. He's believable. What you'll see with Barry, if you listen to some of the albums you'll hear up-tempo things, he's also a swinger. The first thing on the album, the Lambert, Hendricks and Ross thing: 'Cloudburst'—that's brilliant! If you see it done and you hear him, that's sensational! Barry likes jazz. I think if you listen to his albums, you see that it's very versatile.''

Commenting on another aspect of Manilow's artistry, Irv continued, "I think as a composer, I think you will find Barry will be in the next year as hot as Carol Sager is as a writer today. I think you're going to see Barry enjoy that same success. And it will happen on his own recordings, but it'll happen outside too. Somebody is going to come along and pick up some of those Manilow things that are like the fourth cut on the album, you know, it's going to be a single, and they'll have a smash with it. He's that good a writer. I think he's as good a writer as he is a recording artist and producer and performer. I think there are sometimes certain pressures put on the record company, you know, ' ... do it this way ... ' and ' ... do it that way ... ' I give Arista a lot of credit I must say, with Barry's career, they certainly took it to its limit, and I think it's going to grow even larger. God, I don't know how many albums this guy sold last year . . . "

"Well," I inserted, "I know the 'Live' album is 'Platinum' on its way to 'Double Platinum,' so . . . it's incredible!"

"It's incredible," Biegel exclaimed citing other artists to have achieved single album sales of "one million plus," "when you consider . . . Boz Scaggs had a huge one, I think his went 'Double Platinum.' But you don't find many single artists that have sold that kind of album. No, it seems the predominant thing in the music business is the groups who make it to 'Double Platinum.' You know, Boston, and Fleetwood Mac, and Chicago almost is 'Double Platinum' every time out. But, it seems the groups are the ones that are doing 'Double Platinum.' To be a solo artist to do it . . . very difficult! And Barry's one of those guys. But he deserves his success; he's worked hard for it.

"I think the career guidance has been outstanding. I can't say enough about Miles' direction."

On another topic I brought up the recent press release that I had read concerning Manilow's possible entry into the field of motion pictures, "I know there's talk about Universal giving him a screen test.

"Sure!" Biegel exclaimed. "Well, I think, Number One: physically, you know what he is . . . he photographs well . . . he projects! Barry could have done *Portnoy's Complaint* if you wanted him in that role. You know, the Jewish boy from Brooklyn, and I think it's going to be . . . I think Barry will be the male Barbra Streisand! I believe it. I think Barbra Streisand is the biggest star in our business. All aspects of our business, because our business is so intertwined today with film and television, and people crossing over.

"I mean, there are a lot of good performers, but when you talk about a Streisand, and you talk about a Sinatra . . . and people may think I'm crazy . . . if you want to use this quote; I'm going to stick by it: 'I think Barry Manilow can reach that sphere.' That's how much I believe he can do it. Now, as he progresses, his music will change a bit, and I just believe it. And he deserves it . . . he's a nice man. He really *is* a nice man.

"I'll make one final statement. You know, as much as I feel I have been responsible for Barry, to a degree . . . and that's a fact . . . I've got to tell you, I think a talent like that, you know there are a lot of people that help along the way, but I think with those kind of talents, because I think he's very special, really emerge one way or the other. Well, I think maybe I was lucky enough to be in the right place at the right time, and maybe be professional enough to have recognized that. But, I must tell you, we're in a very creative business—but I don't know too many geniuses. I am certainly not one of them. But there are certain kinds of talents, and he happens to be in that category as far as I'm concerned . . . that emerged . . . as you say.

"It's nice the way it happened, because we had a game plan. You know, this was all very well laid out. But I think Barry would have emerged had he been singing on the corner . . . and picked up by 'Do-Wa Records' or whatever, because he was that good. And I think this has been proven."

VI
YOU'VE GOT TO HAVE FRIENDS:
Gurst on Manilow

"Oh, you've got to have friends, to make the day last long . . . " is one of the lines from the Buzzy Linhart/Mark Klingman composition "Friends." Bette Midler recorded the song on her "Divine Miss M" L.P. In addition to the background singers (including Melissa Manchester), Barry Manilow was part of "Miss M's choir" singing on that cut. The song went on to become Bette's trademark song in her live performances, and so sincere was the message of the lyrics, that at the time Barry recorded his first solo album, his own version of the song was included.

Among the closest individuals on Barry's list of "Friends," is a recurring name that appears on all of Manilow's albums—that of Lee Gurst. A long-time acquaintance of Barry's, Lee has predominantly been working as his photographer and as his drummer both on stage and on record. He has handled various instrumental duties on all of Barry's albums and on the first Lady Flash L.P. His photos can be found on the "Tryin' To Get The Feeling" back cover, the front and back of the "This One's For You" album, and the interior stage shot inside of "Barry Manilow Live."

In appreciation for all that they have been

through together, on the inside of "Barry Manilow Live," Barry wrote about the multi-'Platinum' project:

"My very personal thanks to my friend, drummer, photographer, conductor, art director and confidant, Lee Gurst, for his enormous support and talents through the years. Lee, this one's for you."

The first time I spoke to Lee Gurst was on the telephone the same week that I had done my Lady Flash interview. It was at that time that he informed me that he would be going out to California for the summer, and would be back and forth between the West Coast and the East. We made plans to connect at some later point, to sit down and discuss his involvement with Barry Manilow. Lee found it effortlessly easy to become mesmerized with relaxing in the California sunshine. While there, Lee found himself dividing his time between hanging out at the swimming pool of his Los Angeles apartment, and flying around the area, piloting himself about in small private planes. Lee contemplated his first post-Manilow projects after having parted ways careerwise the same time that Lady Flash had.

It was in Los Angeles, the beginning of August that we finally got together. One particular Wednesday afternoon, Lee was out flying a small aircraft he had rented, and I was out driving a car that I had for my week on the coast. Lee landed at the Hawthorne Municipal Airport, having taken off from another local airstrip. I picked him up in my red Cougar, and on our way to the destination of our interview, we discussed amongst other things, the two magazine cover stories that Barry was the subject of that month: *People* and *Crawdaddy*.

Lee is a creative fellow-Libra who divides his time between any one of the dozens of projects that he finds himself involved in. His interests include drumming, photography, flying, writing and directing, and at the time of our meeting, he was unsure of what it was that he would become involved in next.

"I was born in Atlantic City," Lee began, "raised in Atlantic City and the suburbs of Philadelphia. I went to New York to go to college and was hired to do an off-Broadway show for which Barry Manilow was the music director. It was a thing called "Now," an ill-fated little musical at the Cherry Lane Theater, and Barry was the piano player, and I was the drummer. We had a guitar player, and we were the band. And so, we got along very nicely, we liked working together, we hit it off well, and began a string of jobs . . . a series for CBS, a couple of other shows, into the demos, into the jingles, into Bette Midler . . . into Barry's touring, which began for me in October, 1974.

"I started off as friend and drummer . . . and became leader of the band, and then the conductor, and then the photographer, and then the art director. Insinuating my way into a lot of areas, I also contributed to arrangements and lines . . . it was a big family effort on the tours."

When I stated Lady Flash's assertion that Barry's entourage was of parallel positive personalities, Lee said supportively, "The groups were always picked with an eye toward compatibility. At least on a personal level, things were always very comfortable. Everybody got along with everybody else, and it really was an extended family kind of thing. You know, a little band of hearty travelers making their way around the country. Joking with each other at eight o'clock at the airport and consoling each other after losing out on the lady in the front row who didn't show up backstage! Things like that!" he laughed.

"So, it was very much a family effort. I don't know how long things like that can go on. Somewhere along the line things probably changed, that certainly has been the case through this last tour. And so, my Barry Manilow story is lengthy, rather involved. We did a lot of work together, and when we weren't working together, we were able to stay in touch ... some lapses during the years when he was totally wrapped up in traveling with Bette, and I was off doing other things and didn't see him, but we're close friends. That made for stormy working relationships now and again, but that's not unusual. It's probably healthy, although Barry doesn't think so."

Elaborating on the advertising era, Lee explained, "I was involved only as a musician. Barry was coaching a number of singers and playing auditions for a lot of people, and beginning to write some songs. It came time to go in and do a couple of demos for his things, and singing on his demos ... and a few other things.

"I think one of the earliest was ... there were a couple of bank commercials in Pennsylvania, and a couple of tries at a Dodge Charger, which was not bought. They were submitted to the agency, they requested them, and they used the bank commercials in Pennsylvania. One led to another, and after writing a couple, then he began to play piano on them, and then to singing on a couple of them. All of a sudden, once his records started to go, it was, 'Let's get Barry Manilow to do a Kodak commercial!' or something like that . . . 'Barry Manilow for Kodak!' But those things have all but stopped completely. I don't think he's done any commercials for the last year and a half, maybe longer.

"At this point, it can go one of two ways. They either call for Barry Manilow to put his name on a commercial, in which case it's a more expensive proposition for the advertiser; or they call him to be involved anonymously, as he was before, in which case he'd probably want more money to get involved in it. The thing is . . . that Barry likes to have control over his projects, so he'd probably want to produce the commercial. And for one reason or another, this just hasn't worked out. He's been awfully busy and there have been other things to pay attention to besides the commercials. He didn't need the money anymore, and commercials are not the sort of thing that you do because you just love to make commercials. Not that they're not fun, and that they're not a worthwhile craft, but it's just not, 'Gee, I really miss doing commercials . . . I've got to do one!' When you've got albums coming out every year, singles and television shows, I don't imagine you feel the need to stroke yourself with another commercial. So, it just hasn't happened for quite a while. But when it was going on, commercials brought him an incredible amount of freedom.

"Record companies," Lee elaborated, "frequently put up money for tours, things like that, in exchange for which they get shares of publishing. They get longer commitments, they get more albums . . . whatever it may be. They negotiate for it. The money is returned . . . I mean, it's an advance; it's never a gift. But, even though you do pay it back they also get a couple of things here and there. All those commercials that put money in the bank gave Barry the freedom to say, 'I need the money, but not badly enough that I'm going to sign away something I want later.' So, that kept his publishing rights, and it kept a chance to keep a little bit of freedom, a little bit of autonomy.

"So that's where the commercials really paid off. They were an excellent training ground, because you learn the precision of studio work, and you learn how to condense everything for the strongest, most immediate impact . . . when you know how to say something quickly and concisely. You can always expand on it later for songs and longer works. But, at least you know how to do it. You know how to find the important elements, and how to work with them. So commercials were very important for that. They provided good contacts . . . that's how he met Ron Dante, his co-producer. The commercials were worthwhile on a lot of levels.

"He was doing commercials while he was working with Bette, and his first album was recorded while he was still working with Bette. So these things were overlapping. The reason for leaving Bette was . . . when it became time to continue on with her recording career, which seemed to take off very nicely, there was no choice but to say, 'This is where I've got to go.' He'd done what he could do with her, and for her. It was the next obvious step. Like Lady Flash going off on their own: Barry got them started on their recording career, and the choice is to have them stay a back-up group that maybe puts out records now and then, or follow through and become a recording group. And, that means not being a back-up group anymore. That means taking a step out front, and saying, 'We're going to take our shot!' That's what happened with Barry leaving Bette. It was the same situation. They correspond now and again ... they cross paths now and again. Lady Flash stays in touch with Barry. It's a very similar, parallel situation.

Explaining the latest friendly fission, Lee stated, "That 'live' album was our final contribution. We finished up the tour in Las Vegas in April, and everybody bid everybody else a teary farewell, and we all went through a withdrawal ... a tearing-apart thing. We all keep in touch and most of the band is out here, and all of Lady Flash are out here, and that was the end of a cycle. I don't know that some of those people won't work with Barry again, but even if they do, I think April was the end of an era. Even if the entire group goes out with him again, it will be somehow different. I think Barry has arrived ... you know, Barry has changed status a little bit. It's no longer as tenuous as it once was. As with any group or organization, the tone is set at the top. So if Barry goes through a re-adjustment, it will be felt among the people who work with him or for him. So, whether or not they go out with him again, I think it's a wise course ... completing the cycle. I think Lady Flash will go off on their own. I think they'd be the least likely to work with him. I can see where he might hire some of the other people for the tour ... the technical people, maybe some of the band members.

"I don't know ... I don't know what my work situation is with Barry. I think I've done all I can do, and Barry's looking for some new influences, and some new experiences, and I am too. We splash and play in the pool, and that's about it at this point. We basically have been taking time off since April. We closed in Las Vegas and went to the hotel and packed up for three-and-a-half weeks in Hawaii, and back to L.A. to look around a little bit, and back to New York to do some work, to do some work with Barry as a matter of fact. Then back to L.A. and getting a suntan, and flying my airplanes, and enjoying the kind of vacation that I've been saving up for for a long time! I haven't had more than two days off every month for the last two years, so between all the different things I was working on at the time . . . I just never got the chance to stop. Now; I stopped! Now I wake up in the morning and say, 'What do I feel like doing today?' and that's a treat!

"When I decide I've been lazy and just sat around long enough, I got into flying as a project, just to keep the adrenaline going, but this is vacation time. I don't know what I want to get into . . . that's the problem. I can do a lot of different things, and what I'd like to do is start putting them all together, working in production. I kind of think maybe television and films. I really want to have a chance to follow through on a project and influence its outcome, from beginning to end. It was always sort of frustrating for me to play music for someone, and not really be able to suggest that it might be more interesting if we changed the ending . . . or whatever."

About his involvement on Barry's albums, Lee admitted, "I was on the original ('Barry Manilow'), but I never got credit for it. I went in one day when some of those tracks were recorded as demos —whatever it was—the first $5,000 that they decided to sink into demos. I played on, along with a terrific band. I was playing percussion. Those

things were sold—there were four—and I got paid
for it. But, I didn't work that hard. The album was
released with a minimum of credits. They really
didn't list all of the people who played on the thing.
Then, when it was re-released, the group which was
on tour then with him, which was the City Rhythm
Band and Lady Flash, went back and re-recorded
one or two of the songs completely. I added some
things to the existing tracks from the first album.
So, I got credited for the re-release, but I did play
on the first album.

"I wrote in a bio, for one of the concerts
somewhere, that I'd played on four or five albums
at the time, and all but one of the singles. I didn't
play on 'Mandy.' Otherwise, I've played on
everything else to date ... the singles and the
albums. I've got a nice collection of 'Gold' records.
Barry gave 'Gold' records to the group. So, we had
a whole wallful of 'Gold' albums, 'Platinum'
albums and things like that. They're pretty! Gold
sure looks good on the wall! They really do!" he
laughed. "They're very impressive, and the
manager of our building here is very impressed that
we have this wall with 'Gold' albums. It's very
pretty. The 'Platinums' aren't half as pretty as the
'Gold,' but they're worth more! Now they're going
to have to come up with something beyond
'Platinum' like a 'Uranium' record or something!"

"What kind of things went into the 98-city
tour?" I inquired next.

"Blood, sweat, and tears; craziness and insanity
and nerves—a lot of things!" Lee exclaimed. "You
take on something like that ... and it's pretty
heavy! The show that you put together—it doesn't
make any difference whether you put it together

for ninety-eight cities, or ninety-eight countries, or ninety-eight months—you do the same quality of show for one audience. You don't make it better because you can do more audiences. So, we spent ... I think, about four weeks in rehearsals; by the time you include vocal rehearsals, music rehearsals, dance rehearsals, final rehearsals. You put it all together for a week or two, and then you take it on tour, and then you rehearse it some more to polish up the things that you begin to discover once it actually works in front of an audience. I would say about a month of rehearsing. Five weeks is average for the tour, and before that Barry takes himself off somewhere and hides out and tries to dream up something new and unusual to do for the tour.

"This last 98-city thing ... it was long. It dragged on for about nine months! But, toward the end it lightened up a little bit. That was the most difficult of the tours, because Barry Manilow was becoming something much bigger than he had ever started out. That put a lot of pressure on him. He couldn't just go out and eat after a show, and he couldn't just go for a walk in a shopping center if he wanted to. He didn't have the freedom he did before. When you lose that freedom, you begin to feel the pressure of the fans ... and being well-known and recognizable. It's hard to adjust to. I personally wouldn't want it. We had enough singles, and the TV exposure had been heavy enough and the TV special was coming up ... and the concert tours ... God knows they played to a lot of people. By the time you enter that stage, you've got to adjust. Your personal life has to go through an adjustment; you don't have the freedom to go out, like I said. There's no choice but to stay in the hotel, when you'd rather be out shopping for shoes and things."

Lee explains that he and Lady Flash made sure that Barry was entertained in his confinement. "So we tried to make life a little bit easier. You know, we spent time hanging out with Barry, at least he wouldn't be locked in the hotel suite alone. There was that kind of pressure. There was the pressure of maintaining a quality performance night-after-night under sometimes grueling circumstances . . . for a lot of people that were expecting a good show. You know . . . three flights a day to get to some place that should have been saved for another day. You arrive tired and the bus pulls up outside of the theater an hour before the show . . . and you don't have time to check into the hotel, so you don't bother! You go right to the hall and do a sound check, and occasionally you run into problems there, and 'Well, we've got thirteen seconds to fix it before we open the house!' Then you've got to get dressed and this and that. We tried to keep a leisurely pace, tried to arrange for a sound check around five o'clock and to have enough time to eat dinner around six o'clock so we could have enough time to digest it while we dressed. But, the best laid plans of mice and men . . . etcetera . . . etcetera!

"On the other hand," he continued, "it was an incredibly rewarding tour, because we'd gone to cities where we had never been. It's strange to pull into a city like that, where you've barely heard the name of the city . . . or you've never even seen it, and the people yelling and screaming at you as though you were an old friend. That was incredibly satisfying. A lot of people showed up, we never had empty seats, and so while that put a pressure on us, it was also very satisfying to see that kind of thing. Very gratifying. And people were asking for our favorite material from time to time, the things that we considered the really high quality stuff that sometimes is not commercial enough for a single. To find people picking up on that . . . really enjoying it. To get notes from fans: 'I just wanted to let you know that I really enjoyed your music . . . I respect what you do . . . It really means a lot to me . . . It makes me feel good!' "

On the subject of Barry's recordings, we began to discuss the first of Barry's recordings, namely the original version of "Could It Be Magic?" that Barry recorded with the group Featherbed, that was produced by Tony Orlando. In the conversation Lee revealed to me that Barry wasn't 'with' the group Featherbed . . . he *was* the group!

According to Gurst, "In those days it was not common for singer/songwriters to be releasing a lot of things under their own name. A great many groups that have recorded through the years have been one individual. The Archies, The Cufflinks, The Detergents . . . were all Ron Dante! All of them . . . at the same time!"

The most important series of events that appeared in Barry Manilow's career occurred in conjunction with his working with Bette Midler.

"Barry and I would be walking along the street, talking about this crazy singer he was working with at this crazy club," Lee said of his first exposure to Bette. "He wanted me to work with her, but she already had her own group, so that didn't work out. And when they needed someone and hired me as a replacement for a sub; I started working with her. So I was around for that. It was an interesting experience . . . wandering into the path of something like a Bette Midler! He was very impressed with her. I found him devoting a lot of time and energy to coaching her and working with her . . . developing an act. I think he saw something really worth being involved with, and worth building and developing. I did some touring with her. I played for her a couple of times at the Baths, a couple of times as Upstairs At The Downstairs, New Years Eve."

On into the emergence of Barry's own career, I asked Lee if he had been on the spring of 1974 debut tour?

"Not the first time," he answered. "I was in touch and I heard all the horror stories about working with Freddie Hubbard and all that, but I was not involved in the first tour. I went to see him perform at The Bottom Line when I'd finished up the things I'd been working on. It came time for the second tour and he asked me if I was interested. Initially I said 'No,' because I'd just settled down from some traveling. But I loved the music, and I thought it would be fun to work with him, and I decided to do it. And, Miles said, 'No, you've already got somebody. I don't think you should have friends along, it's better if they don't work for you.' So, Barry said 'No.' Fine. Then I settled down again.

"I was helping out with the bass players auditions one day, because the drummer he had hired was not available. I was playing drums with the bass players who were auditioning, and in the middle of the audition, he walked in and said, 'You might as well learn this. I just spoke to Miles, and you're doing the tour.' And that was it!

"I saw his big dress rehearsal at Carroll's. Before the first tour he did a mammoth production in

Carroll's Rehearsal Studios," recalled Gurst. "They brought in lights, they brought in an audience, they brought in video tape equipment, the press, and all that sort of thing—just to try breaking in the show before it went on tour. That kind of thing is never really very wise. It's a very unusual audience. It's not really working conditions. It amounted to a show-off rehearsal. We never did it again; it was never done for the other tours. All the friends were invited down to Carroll's to watch this thing before his first tour in March, 1974. It was interesting. I remember having to leave before it was over. But, it did not pay off. And as I said, we never again rehearsed the show for an audience. We rehearsed ourselves, and when it was ready, we went into the clubs and we used those audiences to make adjustments."

Speaking about Barry's future directions, Lee said from his vantage point, "Well, films are a natural. Films loom on the horizon as something new and challenging. I think everybody likes to find new challenges. Television continues . . . that won't be new. The shows hopefully will be new and creative. To do another recording would not be new, to do another television show will not be new, even though it may be a new type of television show. Films are a new area. Barry has retained his roots and his love for the theater, and I'm sure would like very much to be involved in a Broadway show. Composing a Broadway show—maybe even performing in a Broadway show—I don't know."

I asked a question about Miles Lourie, and about the people around the entire operation that forms the executive structure behind Manilow. Lee explained, "One thing that I would like to see made very clear—Barry gets input from Miles and Clive, and the people around him ... but, Barry manages Barry. Barry is the one who plans his career ... who was thinking of it in terms of longevity and a place in the world of show biz. I think Barry, to a very great extent, is the one who wants to get into these different areas. It's a very personal challenge, and a personal fulfillment. Miles's contributions, important and valid as they may be, I don't think are in artistic areas. They are in business areas.

"Barry as an artist ... Barry as a person ... is very talented, a little bit restless, very creative, and will be looking for new avenues to express himself. So, it will be natural to go very purposefully into other areas. I think films, Broadway, things like that, will be happening sooner than say, five years. There are opportunities waiting to be found. Barry's thinking in those directions, and when the opportunities present themselves—or can be created—he'll be there.

"I would like to see Barry get the credit for picking and choosing a lot of his moves artistically," Lee stressed, "Barry produces his recordings, because he can't be in two places at once, he's got to have another pair of hands and ears to help, but I think Barry hasn't gotten enough credit for the work he's done. He wrote the last special, he conceived the last special, he directed four-fifths of the last special. The choreography that was done on the last special was done by Lady Flash and Barry Manilow. Barry Manilow is a Barry Manilow production, not all the people who put their names on these products!"

Pinpointing the personality behind the productions I asked Lee, "What was Barry like when you first met him; worked on his play? What impressed you about him?"

"Barry was singing at the time, and writing, and beginning to do all the things he would later make a career of," Gurst reflected. "I remember then, just dying for the moment . . . for the time when he would be able to release records. He says he wasn't thinking so much about it. Maybe consciously he wasn't thinking so much about it . . . but it was there waiting to happen."

Lee told of one particular occasion, "The first time we played a concert in Memphis, March, 1975, we had five or six thousand people filling the house . . . yelling and screaming! I remember at the end of the show, the cheers were so overwhelming . . . this was our first big concert. We were just finishing up with nightclubs, and I remember the cheers at the end of the show being so overwhelming that while we were playing whatever the last song was; I was crying during the show! We finished that and did the encore, and again, I was getting a little teary-eyed during the bows, and I got myself all put together. I went back to the dressing room and I said, 'I've been waiting five years for that to happen.' And Barry really didn't know what I was talking about. He honestly didn't know what I was saying, and I said 'I've just been waiting for that for a long, long time!'

"In those years, things were relatively relaxed. He was living in Brooklyn when I first met him, but he soon moved to Manhattan, and he had a little garden in the backyard that he'd never had before. Bagel came along in the early seventies, or late sixties, I don't remember which, probably the late sixties. We were kicking around. I guess you could romanticize it, you know ... the stories of everybody's Greenwich Village years ... and doing the shows, and going to the clubs, and there wasn't an incredible pressure on at that point. There was nothing that *had* to be delivered.

"We were all working. We were scuffling for next month's rent. Barry was, and still is, very much involved with his friends, and at that point there was probably a greater freedom for friendship, because you couldn't want anything from Barry Manilow at that point other than friendship. In those days, he was just the guy who lived next door and played the piano.

"I remember the off-Broadway show. After rehearsals, Adrian Anderson was a good friend at the time ... Marty Panzer was a good friend. Linda Allen was in the picture ... it was beginning to be at that point. We were doing the off-Broadway show. Rehearsals, or between the matinee and evening performance on weekends, we were down in the Village ... and we'd go over to Emilio's and eat out in the garden. Looking back, it was all very pleasant ... very comfortable. Like I said, we were scuffling for the rent. There was a Christmas in the late sixties when I announced I wasn't buying Christmas presents ... I couldn't afford it. I didn't even have the rent paid, let alone buying Christmas cards ... and, I got a $100 check in the mail from Barry! He said, 'I don't want to hear another word about it. You'd do the same for me some day. Buy Christmas cards ... send me a Christmas card. —Barry.' ... and that's the way things went!

" 'The Drunkard' was going on at the time ... it was clicking along and that was a lot of fun! I guess things were really just starting to happen when I came into the picture. The piano-player-in-a-cocktail-lounge things were pretty much over. Barry and Jeanne Lucas were beginning to work around New York quite a bit ... Upstairs At The Downstairs, occasionally at The Improvisation ... I don't know if they actually 'worked' there ... I know one evening in particular we all went over there and they performed.

"In those days we'd bring a whole bunch of instruments into his apartment for Christmas parties, or for get-togethers, and we'd play and sing. Bette got up and sang one day ... and Melissa would sing ... the next-door neighbors would perform Barry's songs ... lots of fun! Like I say, I'm forgetting, pain is a hard thing to remember, so I'm forgetting all about that. I'm forgetting how we used to scuffle and the disappointments of a promising job that didn't come through or something. But, there was a lot of good stuff going on at that point.

"I remember veal marinara at Emilio's ... veal cacciatore ..." he corrected, "every Saturday and Sunday between shows, that would be it ... that was the favorite. Oh, you know ... drifting in and out of the lousy demo studios in New York, where they never really manage to get things on records the way they're supposed to!"

Those sparse days are now all over for Barry and for Lee. The cold winters without money for Christmas are all a thing of the past. Both Barry and Lee will separately be moving on to new projects ... and perhaps their paths will soon again intersect. The climb to the top was a real struggle to deal with some days, but it was well worth the wait, for a taste of the "Sweet Life."

VII
WHAT'S YOUR SIGN?:
Manilow the Gemini

Says Manilow on Manilow: "I have a wall full of 'Gold' records . . . and that's my reward. I'm happy. But, it's a life of hard work; I think I've read about it from every artist who has made it to the top.

"I'm not sociable because I chose not to be. I'm much too busy with my work, first of all. Besides, I don't like parties. I don't like being phony, and I'm not good at small talk."

When it comes to personal relationships with people, Barry often speaks of his girlfriend Linda Allen, "When I want to have fun, I see Linda. Linda's my lady. We play backgammon together, it's relaxing."

Yet, he can turn around and completely contradict himself on another occasion and first profess, "Anybody who really needs to, can get to me," and then, "I'm a very private person. I don't want to share my life with anybody!"

Split personality? A case of duality? Precisely, and so typical of Gemini's. On different occasions their friends will claim they know two completely separate people housed in the same body!

"If," Barry insists of his current popularity, "years ago anybody had told me that all this would be happening to me, I'd have told him he was crazy!" But he admits, "I'm very happy about my success. I'm enjoying every second of it. I never really knew where I'd end up, but I was always prepared for it."

Was Barry always *just* prepared for success, or was he always destined to occupy the position in the performing world that he now finds himself in? According to a couple of reliable sources of predetermined fact-finding it seems that Barry Manilow didn't unconsciously stumble upon success—he naturally gravitated towards it!

Both on my own—and aided—I sought out the influences of the supernatural realms of numerology and of astrology to sketch out Manilow's personality. By taking Barry's birthdate on the 17th of June, that brings into play his signifying numeral of 8. This number is derived by "compounding" the birthdate of 17 into its lowest form (done by adding "1" and "7") thus he is what is known as a "number eight" personality.

Consulting a highly respected book on numerology called *Numbers Will Tell* by Gerun Moore (Tempo Books, 1977), I found out some startlingly coincidental things about Mr. Manilow! The section on "number eights" outlines in part, the facts that . . .

You of the number 8 group are apt to be lonely and misunderstood. You have a compulsion for doing favors for everyone. You should marry late in life and are apt to marry a person younger than yourself. You can be a success or failure. Though you may appear cold to people, you are very warm. You should avoid secret love affairs and stay away from alcoholic beverages. You have the uncanny ability to appear and act sober even though you're ready to fall on your face. Your approach to the opposite sex is dynamic, and though you don't know it, you have many admirers, persons secretly in love with you. You gamble with life, take wild chances and never look to others for guidance since you are quite capable of taking care of your own affairs. You love strange and unbelievable stories and excel at telling jokes. You like to be noticed and can be counted on whenever help is needed.

Delving more specifically, and checking into the exact aspects of 17, the book states ...

This is a number of love and happiness. The beginning of life will be a struggle, but the last half will bring success and joy. Number 17 people have cheerful dispositions and if they so desire, will make a name for themselves and become famous ... This number governs the amusement field. It is the best of the number 8 group.

In order to compose a more "starry-eyed" portrait of Manilow, on a recent rather muggy summer morning in New York, I found myself seated before a coffee table scattered with mutilated sugar packets, deli coffee, two pineapple danishes, and a solar astrological chart of Barry's life. Looking down at the chart, astrologer Don Elam drew analytically, "There's an interesting sidelight here. Mars is in 29° Leo. That's in Conjunction with the Fixed star Regulus. This is also what the ascendant of Franz Liszt, the pianist of the last century, was. Now, I know that Manilow is very much of a

Lisztian figure. He's thin, long-haired . . . the backdrop I've seen on his album where he's playing the
piano reminded me very much of Liszt. So, I think
that Mars is the energy; the outward directed energy and so that seems to be an interesting connec-
tion there with the figure of the past.''

The chart that Elam calculated on was compiled
using his nine-year know-how in the study of astrological phenomena, and certain data that I
provided; namely date, year and place of birth.
From this Elam made his ''solar chartings'' of
Barry's personal and career characteristics and ultimate potentials. Among the statistics we contemplated in conjunction with the stars were project
prospects of his performing career: recordings,
concerts, and even entering into new territorial
challenges . . . including films. We came across
some very interesting findings including Manilow's link with Franz Liszt, the Hungarian com-
poser/pianist who was the ''rage'' of the last century!

Although I recognize Elam as a highly knowl-
edgeable man with his head in the upper strat-
osphere, and a diversified Libran, Don is better
known to the record-listening public as the saxo-
phone-playing member of the Texas rock/
swing/blues band that calls itself Balcones
Fault, originating from Austin, Texas.

In addition to his post with Balcones Fault,
Elam is simultaneously the musical arranger for
the Houston Pops Orchestra, an ensemble that
recently had the distinction of appearing in Carnegie Hall. Says Elam of Balcones Fault, and it's
humorous presentation of serious music, ''Pointing
out perhaps not so much the similarities of all these
different styles, but the fact that they're all en-

joyable and playable, and that you can put it into one evening. You can stretch the concepts so it absolutely blends one into the other; the different styles. Seems to me that eclectic-type assemblages are sort of where it's going," he cited of the band's diversity, and the current trends of the public.

Prior to projection into Barry's astrological charts—according to Don Elam's calculations—a quick course on Zodiacal phenomena:

The perpetual circle in which the nine planets move around the Sun is called the Zodiac and is divided into twelve signs. At the same time, personal astrology takes into consideration four elements: Fire, Earth, Air, and Water. In a person's horoscope, these elements represent psychological conditions. Aspects known as Cardinal, Fixed and Mutable serve as operating agents as far as the processes of initiation, consolidation, or alternation.

In the subject's chart, these characteristics present themselves with the following personality traits:

Fire: zeal and enthusiasm

Earth: practical and conservative

Air: changeable and communicative

Water: emotional

Cardinal Signs: fast-acting, spontaneous

Fixed Signs: deliberate, difficult to move

Mutable Signs: changeable, sometimes combine the characteristics of Fixity and Cardinality

In an alternating fashion, there exists the following delineation:

1. *ARIES* . . . . .Cardinal (Fire)
2. *TAURUS* . . . . Fixed (Earth)
3. *GEMINI* . . . . .Mutable (Air)

4. *CANCER* .... Cardinal (Water)
5. *LEO* .... Fixed (Fire)
6. *VIRGO* .... Mutable (Earth)
7. *LIBRA* .... Cardinal (Air)
8. *SCORPIO* .... Fixed (Water)
9. *SAGITTARIUS* .... Mutable (Fire)
10. *CAPRICORN* .... Cardinal (Earth)
11. *AQUARIUS* .... Fixed (Air)
12. *PISCES* .... Mutable (Water)

An additional factor considered by Don Elam in his charted forecasts of Barry Manilow took into consideration the positioning of the planets at the time of birth. Among the phenomena he found include the following planetary relationships:

Conjunction: when two planets are less than thirty degrees of each other. The nature of such an occurance is "variable."

Square: when two planets are within ninety degrees of each other. The nature of such an unfortunate occurrance is "difficult."

Trine: when two planets are within one-hundred-and-twenty degrees of each other. The nature of such a favorable occurrance is defined as "easy."

"Manilow's chart," drew Elam, "is most interesting. Sun is in Gemini, and the Moon is in Capricorn. So Gemini is outward towards communications, and Capricorn for the Moon . . . the Moon is the application, the Sun is the basic energy." Explaining the relationship of these heavenly bodies, Don furthered that "Capricorn is a directed, ambitious, accomplishing sort of sign. The Sun is in Gemini and his Moon is in Capricorn: ambition, persuasion, analytical fairness and calmness, mental detachment. So we've got the ambition here.

"There's a lot of things in this chart noting ambition and drive. The Moon in opposition to Saturn is very, very strongly related to drive and ambition ... purpose. Also, worry, anxiety, frustration." Don explained that this can be a good aspect of frustration, as it makes for a "perfectionist" personality, and "he really needs to project this. The overall shape of the planets, how they group themselves, you'll notice the Moon is out by itself. Now there's an unusual configuration here. It's called a 'finger of God.' What that is is two other planets that are in the same relationship 150° angle to another planet. And, this happens to be the Sun and Mars, and that's the finger, that's pointing directly at the Moon. In addition to that, we have this Moon/Saturn opposition, so that really puts a lot of emphasis on the Moon.

"It's like all these energies are focused up through the Moon. For an entertainer, I imagine that's very strong, and makes him very dynamic a performer because he's got all that energy; all that personality there. The interesting thing is that when the Moon and Saturn are in opposition and they're in one another's signs, that is the Moon rules Cancer where Saturn is and Saturn rules Capricorn where the Moon is. So they're sort of in one another's homes so-to-speak. This, I expect, would add a touch of detriment. What that amounts to ... Saturn and the Moon are both in their detriment; so it's not exactly a handicap, but it's probably a little extra incentive, a little extra necessity to bring forth the Moon personality. Moon is generally personality expression. The Sun is the essence, which isn't generally visible in a lot of people. It doesn't always show through as far as what's underneath. The energy that goes through the personality, the personality could be different."

As Don explained it, Barry's personality has been shaped in accordance with the needs of the influences of the Moon. Looking into this aspect, he pointed out the fact that, "The Moon is a 'full' Moon-type. It's still in the 'full Moon' phase. Full Moon refers to a search for fulfillment and it has the added sub-phase to go into disseminating which means synthesis. So it's fulfillment through synthesis. It's sort of like his basic personality; half is pursuing his own life. He has both Venus and Mars in Leo, but they're at the opposite ends. Venus is just entered. Venus just entered Leo, and Mars is just leaving Leo. They're right at the outer ends, and Pluto is right in the middle.

"Now, the midpoint between Mars and Venus, is called 'the point of sex.' That's where the person's concept of duality . . . of basic sex-drive, basic libido, is focused. Exactly in the middle, and having Pluto between those, that is, at the mid-point. It's in the relationship of these two planets. All of these distances are measured on a circle. They're an arc, so between 0° Leo and 29°, you just split the difference and it's 14, or 14 ½ and the mid-point is where those two energies combine. That's the basic concept. So if a planet is found at the mid-point of two other planets, that planet is a relating factor between those two.

"Now, Mars and Venus are the male and female archetypes: the yin and the yang. Mars is the male energy; and Venus is the female—the passive, the receptive, aesthetic nature. Pluto is the unknown . . . sort of 'the masses' . . . the outermost planet. It generally refers to masses, movement, masses of people. For an entertainer, this means he's geared toward the masses. This seems to indicate that his libido is concentrated on finding an outlet through projection to the masses . . . which is what he's doing as a performer.

"Pluto is kind of frustrating. It's not personal. It's very impersonal. Venus in conjunction with Saturn probably has to do with his personal relationships. Saturn is restriction, denial, trials, tests. So in terms of Venus in Conjunction with Saturn in the readings, I found a complex emotional nature, and generally, relationships with people who are either much older, or much younger. He's very sensitive, the sensitivity is hurt often and loyalty given when emotional needs are understood. So, it's like he has to be understood, and it's probably very difficult because he has a complex nature. Saturn is the place where your secret fears are. Now, having that in Conjunction with Venus, Venus is the love nature, so it's a sort of a secret fear of this basic insecurity." This all seems to point up Barry's own admission that he finds it difficult to relate on a one-to-one basis with any one person.

"Well, that's the duality there." Elam stressed that although Barry finds it awkward to relate to a singular individual, there is a need to relate to mass quantities of people. As he interpreted, "Venus is more personal, but Pluto is impersonal, so that's a conflict there that definitely shows up in the chart. Also, the Moon is in opposition to Venus, and his emotions and popularity need reassuring. . . aloneness, avoids risk of exposure. Again, the Moon is in opposition to Saturn too. Opposition is awareness. It's a tension on relationships . . . it's very difficult.

"He has Uranus leading the Sun. Uranus is the planet that rises directly in front of the Sun in this chart. And Uranus is the planet of change, revolution; also nervous energy, electrical energy, highly-charged performance energy. So it's like his Sun is being led by a brilliant, revolutionary spirit. In fact, that's sort of what it's saying . . . all the drive, all these things sort of focused on the personality of the Moon. This refers to the essence, the Sun, which is sort of flaming in a sense. I would say that the Moon makes a very close opposition here: 25 to 26, but Venus is just 5 degrees away, so that actually both Venus and Saturn are in conjunction . . . they're both in opposition to the Moon.

"Also we have this 'finger of God' . . . now that's an unusual configuration. That doesn't occur very often. The fact that it has an opposition here makes it all the stronger, so that this is a funnel so-to-speak. Then on the outside, these outer planets; Uranus, Jupiter, and Neptune . . . there's a Trine relationship. A very smooth, harmonious relationship between Uranus and Jupiter. Jupiter is expansion. It's the opposite of Saturn, which is restriction . . . so this harmonious relationship with Uranus brings an expansive sense of newness, originality, also suddenness, a bursting forth of energy. Also, Jupiter makes a Trine with the Sun too. It's close enough so that is good fortune, expansion, vastness, glowing inside. So, that's very positive here, but this is somewhat negative and problematical; so those are two conflicting elements," Don pointed out.

"The Sun receives all this beneficial strength and support and then the Moon and Saturn and Venus here are sort of under the gun. It's a pretty interesting chart . . . the Moon is the only planet that's an Earth sign; so it's something that's in a planet that's an Earth sign—solid, feet on the ground, definite form. So the Moon in effect, takes the solidity; or is the focus for everything else. So a lot of pressure on the personality. I can understand a certain amount of insecurity, because there's so much pressure on him. This is the kind of chart that shows an awful lot of drive and will to accomplish; to be very successful. The lack of Conjunctions . . . there's not many Conjunctions in the chart. Conjunctions are where the planets are together within five or six degrees of one another. That means the energies are brought together, but here they're not . . . they're separated, so generally his energies probably tend to be scattered, go in different directions. Their need is to bring it together."

According to many sources, including from Barry himself, there is more than a likely indication that acting and theater are due to be added to his ever-expanding list of endeavors. Says Manilow, "I'm very strongly considering acting in movies. I could be a terrible actor for all I know. I probably *will* turn out to be a terrible actor—but I'm sure gonna try. I'd never sung before, I'd never performed in front of an audience before, but I've certainly become a very hot draw, haven't I? I guess that this is the time for me to make my move . . . take some risks."

My last question which I posed to Elam was whether there is an acting role in Barry's future:

"What I mentioned about Mars, Pluto and Venus all being in Leo . . . Leo is the theatrical sign," Elam elaborated. "What I would read that as is a sort of theatrical projection of libido or sexual energy . . . directed toward the masses. So, that's the source of his charisma!"

VIII
THE RENAISSANCE MANILOW:
Onward to New Heights

"I hate the word 'Superstar!' I'm just a musician who sings a little." Barry Manilow professed that his dedication to his projects is far more important to him than the so-called "glory."

"I'm up from nowhere—Brooklyn, up from nothing. I've worked hard to get here, and I'm gonna work hard to stay here. I can't sleep at night for the music going round in my head.

"I would be doing this no matter what. I didn't care, when I first started out, about being successful. It never entered my mind. All that concerned me was the need to express myself musically. I had to do it . . . for myself. I would never advise anyone to pursue a career in music unless he or she had something to say. You can't do it for the sake of getting audiences to love you—an ego trip; you've got to do it for yourself! It's either 'art' or 'heart'—as the saying goes. It's so hard. I knew I had to pursue my music, and I had to throw my whole self into it.

"But . . ." he insisted, "my work is not M.O.R. (Middle Of the Road). I'm not Led Zeppelin, but I'm not saccharine either. My music is well thought-out, adult, professional tunes. All I'm really trying to do is bring back intelligent music. I haven't figured out my 'style' yet, and sometimes I wonder if I really do have a 'style'. But I'm on to something that a lot of people are getting off on!"

Critics who like to dissect performers for their arriving at a successful "commercial" formula for turning out hit after hit, seem to find an easy target in Barry. Manilow is undaunted by such barb-like comments, and explains his own personal recipe for a hit record, "It's not as difficult as it seems. The secret's not necessarily in a catchy hook, a simple lyric or a memorable melody. It's the production that makes all the difference. I treat my single records and my album cuts like they're two different worlds. It's two different ways of making records . . . it's a learned craft, a job. The trouble is that a lot of artists are too hung up on the word 'art' and are not willing to compromise to reach the majority of the listening audience. They'll say, 'This is the way I make my albums and if I get a hit single out of it, that's great, and if I don't—too bad.' It's too bad, all right—for them.

"I don't feel that I'm compromising. I've simply learned how to do both jobs. Because of that, I've cornered a large share of the audience who feel at home with artists who make both good albums and good commercial singles.

"Ask any songwriter and you get another answer; there's no system to writing a song. Sometimes the lyrics come first; sometimes the music. It depends. It's impossible to describe. All I knew at the time I began writing was that many performers didn't seem to be saying enough. And too often the lyrics didn't fit the music. I wasn't moved by many performers. Arrangers inspired me more. But, I must admit, The Beatles began to get to me."

Since the road is too hectic for composing, or

even approaching the proper frame of mind to concentrate, Barry does his writing at home in his artistic solitude. On different occasions Barry has claimed that his favorite food is "Hamburger Helper," which stands to reason . . . what artist in the middle of a project has time to cook for himself without losing his train of thought? So, speaking of "personal recipes" here is another of his quick remedies for a mid-artwork appetite:

BARRY MANILOW'S PUFFY EGGS
—White bread slices, lightly toasted
—American cheese sandwich slices
—Eggs, separated
—Paprika
For each serving, cover slice of toast with cheese slices. Beat egg whites until stiff peaks form and spoon onto the cheese slices. Indent center with spoon. Carefully place egg yolk into intentation. Sprinkle with paprika. Place on baking sheet; bake at 350 degrees (F), 15 minutes.

Says Barry: this recipe is perfect for brunches or late-night snacks.

As Barry had revealed when I first met him, he had no intention of stepping out front as a headlining performer. How does he look upon his on-stage role now?

"I still consider it a job," he claims, "because of those many years of being in the background and having to be very solid—the brick, the guy that put it all together. Because of all that discipline, I find it easier to do what I have to do, instead of being the freaked-out artist. I know how to deal with musicians and agents and the public as well. If I were a guitar player they found on the street and made into a star, I might not know how to handle it at all."

Recently Barry and Bagel moved from 'midtown' Manhattan to the 'upper West side,' off of Central Park. The rumor that circulated for a long time was that he would probably re-locate to California. Setting the record straight Manilow maintains, "Everybody in the music business lives out in L.A., but I'm not coming. I chose to live in New York. I'm a city kid with soot in my blood."

At this point in his career, his realm has encompassed a great many people, places and things. In the span of three fleeting years, Barry Manilow has already been through Bagel, Biegel, Bell, Baths, Band-Aids, Mandy, Midler, Magic, Melissa and McDonald's . . . and that's most evidently only the beginning.

Little did he suspect, but this very special gentleman from Brooklyn has been a rider to the stars from the first. The 1970's are but daybreak for this studio musician with a forte for making beautiful music. Thanks to all of his friends and followers, who always seemed to know that one of those days there would eventually be something coming up for Barry, and set out their supportive vibes to help him along—he has arrived.

Barry Manilow, "this one's for you" . . . because you pen, perform, play, and platinum-plate the songs that the whole world sings!

Record mogul Don Kirshner (left) discusses Manilow's career
with author Mark Bego (right). Says Kirshner of Barry's future in
films, ''He obviously is bright, he's got a lot of stage presence,
he knows how to handle people, he's paid his dues, so I think
he can make it!''   Photo: DAVID SIZE

BARRY MANILOW DISCOGRAPHY

Albums:

BARRY MANILOW (BELL RECORDS)
—Released Fall 1973
—Produced by: Barry Manilow and Ron Dante

BARRY MANILOW I (ARISTA RECORDS)
—Released June 1975
—Re-released version of "BARRY MANILOW" (BELL RECORDS)

Side One:
—"Sing It"
(Music and Lyrics by: Barry and Grandpa Joe Manilow)
—"Sweetwater Jones"
(Music and Lyrics by: Barry Manilow)
—"Cloudburst"
(Music and Lyrics by: Leroy Kirkland, Jimmy Harris and Jon Hendricks)
—"One Of These Days"
(Music and Lyrics by: Barry Manilow)
—"Oh My Lady"
(Music and Lyrics by: Barry Manilow and Adrienne Anderson)
—"I Am Your Child"
(Music and Lyrics by: Barry Manilow and Marty Panzer)

Side Two:
—"Could It Be Magic?"
(Music and Lyrics by: Barry Manilow, Adrienne Anderson, and F. Chopin)
—"Seven More Years"
(Music and Lyrics by: Barry Manilow and Marty Panzer)

—"Flashy Lady"
(Music and Lyrics by: Ron Dante and Marty Panzer)
—"Friends"
(Music and Lyrics by: Buzzy Linhart and Mark Klingman)
—"Sweet Life"
(Music and Lyrics by: Barry Manilow)

BARRY MANILOW II (BELL RECORDS)
—Released Fall 1974
—Produced by: Barry Manilow and Ron Dante

Side One:
—"I Want To Be Somebody's Baby"
(Music and Lyrics by: Barry Manilow and Enoch Anderson)
—"Early Morning Strangers"
(Music and Lyrics by: Barry Manilow and Hal David)
—"Mandy"
(Music and Lyrics by: Scott English and Richard Kerr)
—"The Two Of Us"
(Music and Lyrics by: Barry Manilow and Marty Panzer)
—"Something's Comin' Up"
(Music and Lyrics by: Barry Manilow)

Side Two:
—"It's A Miracle"
(Music and Lyrics by: Barry Manilow and Marty Panzer)
—"Avenue C"
(Music and Lyrics by: B. Clayton, J. Hendricks and D. Lambert)

—"My Baby Loves Me"
  (Music and Lyrics by: S. Moy, W. Stevenson
  and I. Hunter)
—"Sandra"
  (Music and Lyrics by: Barry Manilow and
  Enoch Anderson)
—"Home Again"
  (Music and Lyrics by: Barry Manilow and
  Marty Panzer)

"TRYIN' TO GET THE FEELING" (ARISTA
RECORDS)
  —Released October, 1975
  —Produced by: Barry Manilow and Ron Dante

Side One:
—"New York City Rhythm"
  (Music by: Barry Manilow
  Lyrics by: Marty Panzer)
—"Tryin' To Get The Feeling Again"
  (Music and Lyrics by: David Pomeranz)
—"Why Don't We Live Together"
  (Music and Lyrics by: Peter Thom and Phil
  Galdston)
—"Bandstand Boogie"
  (Music by: C. Albertine, Les Elgart, Bob
  Horn and Larry Elgart
  Special Lyrics by: Barry Manilow and Bruce
  Sussman)
—"You're Leaving Too Soon"
  (Music by: Barry Manilow
  Lyrics by: Enoch Anderson)
—"She's A Star"
  (Music by: Barry Manilow
  Lyrics by: Enoch Anderson)

Side Two:
—"I Write The Songs"
  (Music and Lyrics by: Bruce Johnson)
—"As Sure As I'm Standin' Here"
  (Music by: Barry Manilow
  Lyrics by: Adrienne Anderson)
—"A Nice Boy Like Me"
  (Music by: Barry Manilow
  Lyrics by: Enoch Anderson)
—"Lay Me Down"
  (Music and Lyrics by: Larry Weiss)
—"Beautiful Music"
  (Music by: Barry Manilow
  Lyrics by: Marty Panzer)

THIS ONE'S FOR YOU (ARISTA RECORDS)
—Released July, 1976
—Produced by: Barry Manilow and Ron Dante

Side One:
—"This One's For You"
  (Music by: Barry Manilow
  Lyrics by: Marty Panzer)
—"Daybreak"
  (Music by: Barry Manilow
  Lyrics by: Adrienne Anderson)
—"You Oughta Be Home With Me"
  (Music by: Barry Manilow
  Lyrics by: Adrienne Anderson)
—"Jump Shout Boogie"
  (Music by: Barry Manilow
  Lyrics by: Barry Manilow and Bruce
  Sussman)
—"Weekend In New England"
  (Music and Lyrics by: Randy Edelman)

Side Two:
—"Riders To The Stars"
  (Music by: Barry Manilow
  Lyrics by: Adrienne Anderson)
—"Let Me Go"
  (Music by: Barry Manilow
  Lyrics by: Marty Panzer)
—"Looks Like We Made It"
  (Music by: Richard Kerr
  Lyrics by: Will Jennings)
—"Say The Words"
  (Music and Lyrics by: Barry Manilow)
—"All The Time"
  (Music by: Barry Manilow
  Lyrics by: Barry Manilow and Marty Panzer)
—"See The Show Again"
  (Music by: Barry Manilow
  Lyric by: Adrienne Anderson)

BARRY MANILOW LIVE (ARISTA RECORDS)
  —Released May, 1977
  —Produced by: Barry Manilow and Ron Dante

  ACT I—Side 1
  —"Riders To The Stars"
    (Music and Lyrics: Barry Manilow and Adrienne Anderson)
  —"Why Don't We Live Together"
    (Music and Lyrics by: Peter Thom and Phil Galston)
  —"Looks Like We Made It"
    (Music and Lyrics by: Richard Kerr and Will Jennings)

—"New York City Rhythm"
(Music and Lyrics by: Barry Manilow and Marty Panzer)

Side Two:
—"A Very Strange Medley (V.S.M.)"
   A. "Kentucky Fried Chicken"
      (Music and Lyrics by: Al Gorgoni and Rob Nolan)
   B. "State Farm Insurance"
      (Music and Lyrics by: Barry Manilow and Jerry Gavin)
   C. "Stridex"
      (Music and Lyrics by: Barry Manilow)
   D. "Band-Aids"
      (Music and Lyrics by: Barry Manilow)
   E. "Bowlene"
      (Music and Lyrics by Barry Manilow and Lois Wise)
   F. "Dr. Pepper"
      (Music and Lyrics by: Randy Newman and Jake Holmes)
   G. "Pepsi"
      (Music and Lyrics by: Ellen Starr and Joe McNeil)
   H. "McDonald's"
      (Music and Lyrics by Kevin Gavin and Sid Woloshin)
—"Jump Shout Boogie Medley"
   A. "Jump Shout Boogie"
      (Music and Lyrics by: Barry Manilow and Bruce Sussman)
   B. "Avenue C"
      (Music and Lyrics by: B. Clayton, Jon Hendricks and Dave Lambert)

C. "Jumpin' At The Woodside"
(Music and Lyrics by: Jon Hendricks and Count Bassie)
D. "Cloudburst"
(Music and Lyrics by: Leroy Kirkland, Jimmy Harris and Jon Hendricks)
E. "Bandstand Boogie"
(Music and Lyrics by: Barry Manilow, Bob Horn, Les Elgart, Larry Elgart, C. Albertine and Bruce Sussman)
—"This One's For You"
(Music and Lyrics by: Barry Manilow and Marty Panzer)

Side Three:
—"Beautiful Music (Part I)"
(Music and Lyrics by: Barry Manilow and Marty Panzer)
—"Daybreak"
(Music and Lyrics by: Barry Manilow and Adrienne Anderson)
—"Lay Me Down"
(Music and Lyrics by: Larry Weiss)
—"Weekend In New England"
(Music and Lyrics by: Randy Edelman)
—"Studio Musician"
(Music and Lyrics by: Rupert Holmes)

Side Four:
—"Beautiful Music (Part II)"
(Music and Lyrics by: Barry Manilow and Marty Panzer)
—"Could It Be Magic?"
(Music and Lyrics by: Barry Manilow, Adrienne Anderson and F. Chopin)

—"Mandy"
(Music and Lyrics by: Scott English and Richard Kerr)
—"It's A Miracle"
(Music and Lyrics by: Barry Manilow and Marty Panzer)
—"It's Just Another New Year's Eve"
(Music and Lyrics by: Barry Manilow and Marty Panzer)
—"I Write The Songs"
(Music and Lyrics by: Bruce Johnson)
—"Beautiful Music (Part III)"
(Music and Lyrics by: Barry Manilow and Marty Panzer)

Singles:
"Could It Be Magic?" By: Featherbed (Bell Records)
   —Note: All vocals by: Barry Manilow
"Sweetwater Jones" (Bell Records)
"Let's Take Some Time To Say Good-bye" (Bell Records)
   (Music and Lyrics by: Artie Schreck)
   —Note: Released as a single only.
"Mandy" (Bell Records)
"It's A Miracle" (Bell Records)
"Could It Be Magic?" (Arista Records)
"I Write The Songs" (Arista Records)
"Tryin' To Get The Feeling" (Arista Records)
"This One's For You" (Arista Records)
"Weekend In New England" (Arista Records)
"Looks Like We Made It" (Arista Records)
"Daybreak" (Arista Records)

LADY FLASH — "BEAUTIES IN THE NIGHT" (R.S.O. Records)

—Released Summer 1976
—Produced by: Barry Manilow and Ron Dante
  Arranged By: Barry Manilow

Side One:
—"The Thunderbolt"
  (Music and Lyrics by: Barry Manilow and
  Adrienne Anderson)
—"Street Singin' "
  (Music and Lyrics by: Barry Manilow and
  Adrienne Anderson)
—"Never Gonna Let You Get Away"
  (Music and Lyrics by: Barry Manilow
  Solo by: Monica Burruss)
—Medley:
  "Green Plant"
  (Music and Lyrics by: Mitch Margo, P.
  Margo, H. Medress and J. Seigel)
  "Right Now If You Believe"
  (Music and Lyrics by: J. C. White)

Side Two:
—"Jumpin' At The Woodside"
  (Music and Lyrics by: Count Basie, John
  Hendricks)
—"Nowhere To Run"
  (Music and Lyrics by: Eddie Holland,
  Lamonte Dozier, and Brian Holland)
—"Arms Of Mary"
  (Music and Lyrics by: Iain Sutherland
  Solo by: Reparata)
—"Buried In The Ruins Of Love"
  (Music and Lyrics by: Barry Manilow
  Solo by: Debra Byrd)
—"Upfront"
  (Music and Lyrics by: Barry Manilow and
  Bruce Sussman)

ABOUT THE AUTHOR

Mark Bego is an international entertainment writer who has contributed to the pages of *Billboard, Celebrity, Record World, TV Mirror, Rock,* and currently for *Us*.

Born on 'The Cusp' of Libra in Pontiac, Michigan, Bego is a graduate of Central Michigan University, and has a B.A. in the areas of Journalism, Drama, and Broadcasting.

Thus far, Bego has been a Broadway reviewer, a music critic, a contract assistant, a personal secretary, a publicity director, an interviewer, and an assembly line worker. He's also acted, authored, painted, modeled, and photographed.

Bego is also the author of *The Captain and Tennille* (Tempo Books) and is working on an upcoming project with Mary Wilson of The Supremes.